Lupus

Titles in the Diseases and Disorders series include:

Acne
AIDS
Alzheimer's Disease
Anorexia and Bulimia
Anthrax
Arthritis
Asthma
Attention Deficit Disorder
Autism
Bipolar Disorder
Birth Defects
Brain Tumors
Breast Cancer
Cerebral Palsy
Chronic Fatigue Syndrome
Cystic Fibrosis
Deafness
Diabetes
Down Syndrome
Dyslexia
Epilepsy
Fetal Alcohol Syndrome
Food Poisoning
Headaches
Heart Disease

Hemophilia
Hepatitis
Leukemia
Lou Gehrig's Disease
Lyme Disease
Mad Cow Disease
Malaria
Measles and Rubella
Multiple Sclerosis
Obesity
Ovarian Cancer
Parkinson's Disease
Phobias
SARS
Schizophrenia
Sexually Transmitted
    Diseases
Sleep Disorders
Smallpox
Teen Depression
West Nile Virus

DISEASES & DISORDERS

LUPUS

Melissa Abramovitz

LUCENT BOOKS

An imprint of Thomson Gale, a part of The Thomson Corporation

Detroit • New York • San Francisco • New Haven, Conn. • Waterville, Maine • London

© 2008 Thomson Gale, a part of The Thomson Corporation.

For more information, contact
Lucent Books
27500 Drake Rd.
Farmington Hills, MI 48331-3535
Or you can visit our Internet site at http://www.gale.com

Library of Congress Cataloging-in-Publication Data

Abramovitz, Melissa, 1954-
  Lupus / by Melissa Abramovitz.
    p. cm. -- (Diseases and disorders)
  Includes bibliographical references and index.
  ISBN 978-1-59018-999-3 (hardcover)
  1. Systemic lupus erythematosus--Juvenile literature. I. Title.
  RC924.5.L85A36 2008
  616.7'72--dc22

                            2007040394

ISBN-10: 1-59018-999-X

Table of Contents

"The Most Difficult Puzzles Ever Devised"

Charles Best, one of the pioneers in the search for a cure for diabetes, once explained what it is about medical research that intrigued him so. "It's not just the gratification of knowing one is helping people," he confided, "although that probably is a more heroic and selfless motivation. Those feelings may enter in, but truly, what I find best is the feeling of going toe to toe with nature, of trying to solve the most difficult puzzles ever devised. The answers are there somewhere, those keys that will solve the puzzle and make the patient well. But how will those keys be found?"

Since the dawn of civilization, nothing has so puzzled people—and often frightened them, as well—as the onset of illness in a body or mind that had seemed healthy before. A seizure, the inability of a heart to pump, the sudden deterioration of muscle tone in a small child—being unable to reverse such conditions or even to understand why they occur was unspeakably frustrating to healers. Even before there were names for such conditions, even before they were understood at all, each was a reminder of how complex the human body was, and how vulnerable.

While our grappling with understanding diseases has been frustrating at times, it has also provided some of humankind's most heroic accomplishments. Alexander Fleming's accidental discovery in 1928 of a mold that could be turned into penicillin has resulted in the saving of untold millions of lives. The isolation of the enzyme insulin has reversed what was once a death sentence for anyone with diabetes. There have been great strides in combating conditions for which there is not yet a cure, too. Medicines can help AIDS patients live longer, diagnostic tools such as mammography and ultrasounds can help doctors find tumors while they are treatable, and laser surgery techniques have made the most intricate, minute operations routine.

This "toe-to-toe" competition with diseases and disorders is even more remarkable when seen in a historical continuum. An astonishing amount of progress has been made in a very short time. Just two hundred years ago, the existence of germs as a cause of some diseases was unknown. In fact it was less than 150 years ago that a British surgeon named Joseph Lister had difficulty persuading his fellow doctors that washing their hands before delivering a baby might increase the chances of a healthy delivery (especially if they had just attended to a diseased patient)!

Each book in Lucent's Diseases and Disorders series explores a disease or disorder and the knowledge that has been accumulated (or discarded) by doctors through the years. Each book also examines the tools used for pinpointing a diagnosis, as well as the various means that are used to treat or cure a disease. Finally, new ideas are presented—techniques or medicines that may be on the horizon.

Frustration and disappointment are still part of medicine, since not every disease or condition can be cured or prevented. But the limitations of knowledge are being pushed outward constantly; the "most difficult puzzles ever devised" are finding challengers every day.

No Longer
A Death Sentence

Until recently a diagnosis of lupus was considered a death sentence. One study conducted in the 1950s at Johns Hopkins University in Baltimore, Maryland, found that fewer than 50 percent of all lupus patients were alive four years after diagnosis. This has changed in recent years due to more effective treatments. Still, a diagnosis of lupus is a difficult one to receive, and many people think the worst when such a diagnosis is made.

Kelly, a lupus patient, reveals that this pessimism is not always warranted:

> When the doctor said I had lupus, my mother cried. She had an aunt who had died very young from lupus many years ago. My doctor said that, for one thing, things had gotten a lot better and, for another, we shouldn't believe any horror stories that we heard about lupus. Just because something bad happened to someone else doesn't mean that my case is going to be like hers. As it turned out, my case has been pretty mild.[1]

Not all patients have mild cases like Kelly; indeed there are many with moderate to severe cases that can be life threatening. But thanks to modern medical treatments, the Lupus Foundation of America reports that 80 to 90 percent of people with lupus can expect to live a normal life span. There is still no cure for the disease, however, and available treatments have many unpleasant and dangerous side effects, so the fight against lupus has not yet been won.

Researchers are busy investigating the causes and treatments for lupus, and doctors continue to search for ways of making life easier for people who suffer from the disease. They are also investigating why women get this disorder much more often than men and why people of some races get the disease more frequently than others.

Although it is not an automatic death sentence in this day and age, lupus is still an unpredictable disease that poses an ongoing challenge to the people it affects. As Erin, who has had the disease for eleven years, explains:

> Influenza season is here again and most people dread the thought that they might succumb to it. Everyone knows what it's like: the muscle and joint aches, the fever, the fatigue that makes you want to stay in bed forever…. Flu sufferers can console themselves that at least this feeling won't last forever; they will likely feel better in a matter of days. But what if it did last forever? How would that change their lives? … With lupus I don't know how I'm going to feel from minute to minute, because that's how fast it can change. I might be sitting in class or talking with

Skin rashes are a common symptom of some forms of lupus.

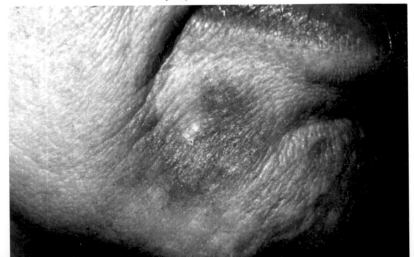

friends when suddenly I feel incredibly sick. Sometimes it feels like the room starts to spin, my vision blurs, I feel nauseated and the pain in my head can be overwhelming … Sometimes I will suddenly get hives all over my body and feel sick all over, or my eyelids and face will swell as if I had just been stung by a bee. Other times I will suddenly feel so exhausted that I can hardly move…. This is not only frustrating, it's also very frightening. The unpredictability of lupus is one of the greatest challenges lupus patients face.[2]

Currently there are hundreds of research projects in the works to try to understand lupus and make living with the disease less of a challenge. There are organizations dedicated to providing lupus patients with support as they navigate through life with this complicated disease. There is reason to hope that those who struggle to control lupus today may be able to reap the benefits of a cure sometime in the future. As the Lupus Foundation of America says, "New research brings unexpected findings each year. The progress made in treatment and diagnosis during the last decade has been greater than that made over the past 100 years. It is therefore a sensible idea to maintain control of a disease that tomorrow may be curable."[3]

CHAPTER ONE

What Is Lupus?

Lupus is the common name for the chronic disease known as lupus erythematosus. The word lupus is Latin for wolf. The reasons this name was attached to the disease are unclear. Some say it was chosen for the disease because the characteristic rash and skin lesions look like bites from a wolf. Another explanation sometimes given is that the butterfly-shaped rash seen on the cheeks and nose of lupus patients resembles the facial markings on a wolf. Several other explanations are offered but the definitive answer is lost to history. Erythematosus, the other part of the disease's name, means red.

Descriptions of lupus date back to Hippocrates (ca. 460–ca. 377 B.C.E.), a doctor in ancient Greece known as the father of medicine, who described a rash that appeared on the cheeks and nose of patients. It was not until 1851 that the disease received its technical name, lupus erythematosus, from the

A distinctive butterfly-shaped rash on the face (also called a malar rash) is one of many signs doctors use to diagnose lupus.

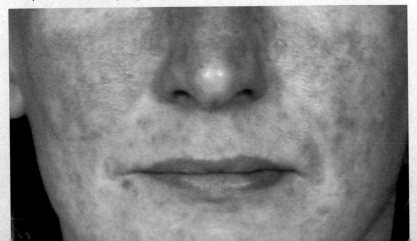

Hippocrates

The Greek doctor Hippocrates is credited with first describing lupus in about 400 b.c. Hippocrates was born on the island of Cos, Greece in 460 b.c. and studied under his father, a physician. He traveled extensively before returning to Cos and opening a medical school. Unlike most authorities in the ancient world, Hippocrates believed that illness was caused by physical or environmental problems rather than by possession by evil spirits or disfavor of the gods. He was one of the first to observe that illness could result from weather conditions or from substances like bad drinking water. He also believed that disease resulted from an imbalance in four bodily fluids, which he called humors; blood, phlegm, black bile, and yellow bile. He believed that the environment and the glands in the body could influence these four humors. Although modern medicine has rejected the concept of humors, some of Hippocrates' ideas remain valid.

He wrote extensively on medical symptoms and treatments in ten volumes of books and in an encyclopedia of medicine and surgery. Because of his extensive insights and works, he is often called the "Father of Medicine." Hippocrates is also known for his Hippocratic oath, a pledge he developed for physicians in training at his medical school. Today physicians take the Hippocratic oath as they begin their practice of medicine.

The Greek physician Hippocrates, also called the "father of medicine," described lupus in about 400 B.C.E.

Types of Lupus	
Type of Lupus	**Affected Body Area**
Systemic lupus erythemato-sus (SLE)	Skin, joints, kidneys, heart, lungs, liver, nervous system, blood vessels, and brain
Discoid lupus erythematosus (DLE)	Just skin
Drug-induced lupus erythematosus (DILE)	Skin, joints, lungs, liver, blood vessels, and brain
Neonatal lupus	Heart and skin

Source: Womenshealth.gov. Available online at: http://www.4women.gov/faq/lupus.htm

French doctor Pierre Cazenave. When Cazenave named the disorder lupus erythematosus, he thought it affected only the skin. But later on, between 1895 and 1903, Sir William Osler of Johns Hopkins University in Baltimore, Maryland, wrote detailed descriptions of lupus that showed that internal organs, as well as the skin, could be involved. The official name of the disease was then changed to systemic lupus erythematosus. The word systemic refers to the fact that some forms of lupus can affect multiple organ systems.

Types of Lupus

When people speak of lupus they are generally referring to systemic lupus erythematosus, or SLE, even though there are actually several other types of lupus that have been defined over the years. There are two subtypes of SLE: non-organ threatening disease and organ threatening disease. In non-organ threatening disease, patients have achiness, fatigue, pain on taking a deep breath, fever, swollen glands, rashes, and swollen joints. Internal organs are not involved in this subtype of SLE, which affects about 35 percent of lupus patients and which does not affect life expectancy. The second subtype of SLE, organ threatening disease, can involve the heart, lungs, kidneys, liver, and

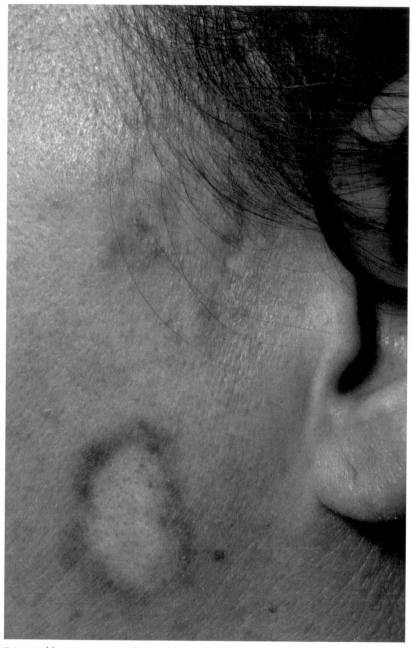

Discoid lesions are scaly patches of skin shaped like ovals. They are found where the skin is exposed to sunlight, like on the face or arms.

blood and affects about 35 percent of lupus patients. This type of SLE is life threatening.

SLE affects women much more frequently than men and affects African Americans, Latinos, American Indians, and Asians more than Caucasians. SLE affects nearly one million people in the United States, of which 80 to 92 percent are women and 90 percent of those women are between the ages of fifteen and forty-five.

Besides SLE there are a few other types of lupus. One is cutaneous (affecting the skin), also known as discoid (disk-like lesion) lupus erythematosus, or DLE. This type affects only the skin and involves about 10 percent of lupus sufferers. It is not life threatening. Another is called drug-induced lupus erythematosus (DILE) and results from taking certain prescription drugs. DILE affects the same number of men as women and is very rare among African Americans. DILE usually starts at about age sixty, is less severe than SLE, and disappears after the offending drug is discontinued.

A fourth type of lupus is called neonatal lupus. This type affects some babies born to mothers with lupus. The baby develops a rash and some heart and blood abnormalities that disappear within about six months. Once these symptoms disappear, the baby no longer has lupus.

Unlike DILE and neonatal lupus, which tend to go away after the offending drug is discontinued or after the baby matures somewhat, most forms of lupus are chronic; that is they do not go away once a person has them, although symptoms may change and become more or less active.

Symptoms of Lupus

Depending on what type of lupus a patient has, symptoms vary. Within the same type of lupus, symptoms may also vary, as explained by the National Institute of Arthritis and Musculoskeletal and Skin Diseases:

> Lupus is a disease that can affect many parts of the body.
> Everyone reacts differently. One person with lupus may

have swollen knees and fever. Another person may be tired all the time or have kidney trouble. Someone else may have rashes. Lupus can involve the joints, the skin, kidneys, the lungs, the heart and/or the brain. If you have lupus, it may affect two or three parts of your body. Usually, one person doesn't have all the possible symptoms.[4]

Although symptoms vary among individuals, according to the author of *The Lupus Book*, "The most common initial complaint in early lupus is joint pain or swelling (in 50 percent of patients), followed by skin rashes (20 percent) and malaise or fatigue (10 percent)."[5] Other common symptoms include fever, loss of appetite, weight loss, skin ulcerations, mouth sores, and hair loss. Inflammation of the blood vessels resulting in Raynaud's phenomenon is often seen in lupus. In Raynaud's

The fingers of a person with Raynaud's phenomenon will turn white, blue, or red in response to stress, cold, or vibration.

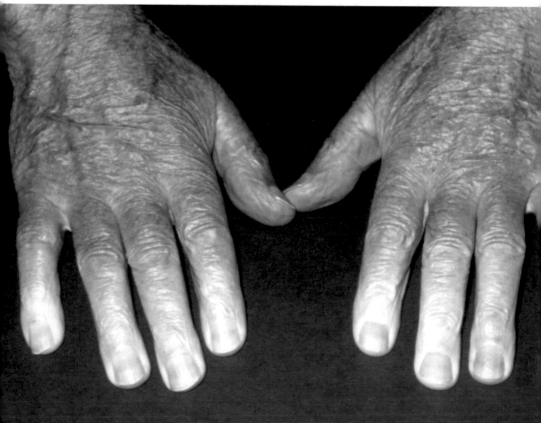

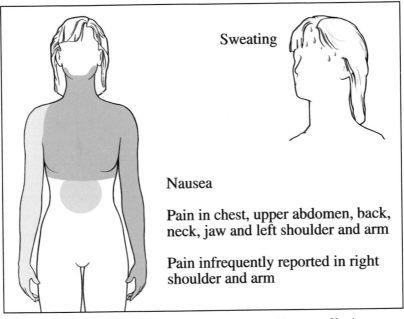

Sweating

Nausea

Pain in chest, upper abdomen, back, neck, jaw and left shoulder and arm

Pain infrequently reported in right shoulder and arm

Many patients with the life-threatening type of lupus suffer heart attacks. Symptoms include sweating, nausea, and pain in the chest, back, neck, jaw, and left shoulder and arm.

phenomenon the fingers turn red, white, or blue in response to stress, cold, or vibration.

Many lupus patients experience shortness of breath and pain on taking a deep breath. Later on in the disease process, problems with the lungs sometimes worsen and patients experience bleeding in the lungs or high blood pressure in the lungs, both of which can be fatal. Many lupus patients have a high heart rate. A prolonged high heart rate can lead to the heart pumping blood less efficiently. This means that other parts of the body may not receive enough oxygen and may not be able to function normally. A high heart rate can also result in the heart requiring more oxygen than normal and thus leaving a patient feeling out of breath or with chest pain. Some experience various other heart problems such as chest pain due to inflammation of the sac surrounding the heart. Others have pain due to inflammation of the heart muscle itself. An inflamed heart muscle does not work properly and can lead to an insufficient amount of blood being pumped into the arteries and body tissues. This can lead to organ failure in various body organs. An inflamed heart muscle can also result in congestive heart failure. Congestive heart failure happens when one side of the heart fails to pump enough blood. This can be a life threatening condition for lupus sufferers because the heart can stop beating at any time. Common symptoms of congestive heart failure include weight gain, swelling of the feet and ankles, swelling of the abdomen, nausea and vomiting, shortness of breath, difficulty sleeping, fatigue, weakness, faintness, rapid pulse, decreased alertness, cough, and decreased urine production. Many lupus patients also experience heart attacks due to damage from the disease and due to high blood pressure or high cholesterol. A heart attack occurs when a blood clot in the artery leading to the heart blocks the supply of blood and oxygen to the heart,

Systemic Lupus Erythematosus involves internal organs like the heart, kidneys, liver, and lungs. When internal organs are involved, the disease can be life threatening.

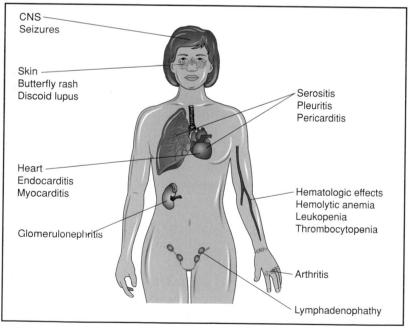

leading to chest pain, shortness of breath, discomfort in the arms, shoulders, neck, and back; and sometimes nausea, vomiting, dizziness, and sweating.

Lupus can also produce changes in the brain that may lead to cognitive dysfunction (not thinking clearly), where the patient shows confusion, difficulty remembering things, and difficulty articulating thoughts. Headaches, seizures, altered consciousness such as coma or excessive sleepiness, paralysis, or other conditions may also appear in lupus. Many patients suffer from depression. Some patients become psychotic (lose touch with reality), have a stroke, experience visual changes, or have numbness or tingling in the hands or feet. Some of these nervous system problems are due to an inflammation of the brain's blood vessels known as vasculitis of the central nervous system. Others, such as vision problems, may be related to lupus's affect on the eye muscles or on the retina of the eye.

Many lupus patients have problems with their gastrointestinal system. Heartburn is common. This is where acid from the stomach flows up into the esophagus and causes burning and scarring. Some lupus patients experience pancreatitis, an inflammation of the pancreas. It can involve pain in the abdomen, swelling in the abdomen, nausea and vomiting, fever, and rapid pulse. Pancreatitis can lead to heart, lung, or kidney failure, all of which can result in death. If bleeding occurs in the pancreas, this can also be fatal.

Problems with the kidneys are also common in lupus. The medical term for kidney malfunction that occurs in lupus patients is lupus nephritis. The kidneys are responsible for filtering and excreting wastes from the body. When they do not work properly, large amounts of protein are secreted in the urine and toxins build up in other parts of the body. Sometimes kidney inflammation produces no symptoms. Other times it can lead to high blood pressure, swollen ankles or shins, fatigue, nosebleeds, foaming urine, confusion, or nausea. Tiffany, a lupus patient, had no symptoms of kidney disease but turned out to have inflamed kidneys. As she revealed:

A few months after I was diagnosed with lupus, my doctor did a urinanalysis and it showed an abundance of red blood cells, and so then I had a kidney biopsy that showed severe kidney inflammation. My kidneys were functioning, but they would have shut down pretty soon if my doctor didn't act quickly. Detecting kidney disease early is key to living a normal life, so I'm very grateful that it was discovered right away.[6]

Lupus sufferers also have abnormal blood cell counts. About 80 percent of SLE patients have anemia, or a low red blood cell count, rendering them pale, tired, and weak. Fifty percent develop low white blood cell counts, resulting in decreased resistance to infection. Many lupus patients also have low blood platelet counts. Since platelets are responsible for blood clotting, low platelet counts can lead to internal bleeding.

Many lupus patients develop Sjogren's syndrome, a condition characterized by dry mouth and dry eyes. This can result

The skin lesions characteristic of discoid lupus are often misdiagnosed as leprosy.

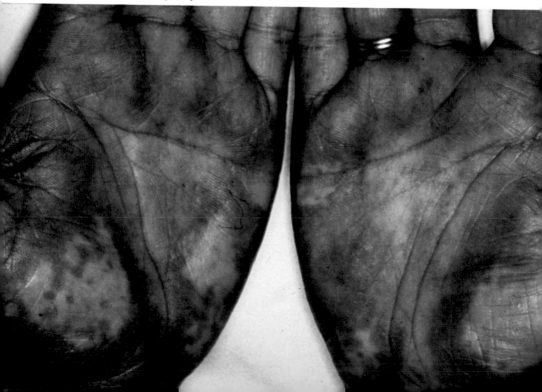

in gum disease, cold sores, tooth decay, impaired vision, and injury to the cornea (the outer layer of the eye).

As noted by the Lupus Foundation of America, all of these diverse symptoms of lupus share the characteristic of inflammation of various body tissues: "Inflammation is considered the hallmark, or primary feature, of lupus: the word is from the Latin word for 'set on fire,' so lupus is characterized by pain, heat, redness, swelling and loss of function, either on the inside or on the outside of the body (or both)."[7]

Difficulties in Diagnosis

Because lupus can involve so many different parts of the body, it can mimic other diseases and is often called "the great imitator." For this reason lupus can be very difficult to diagnose. Lupus can easily be misdiagnosed as thyroid disease, where a patient has too much thyroid hormone. Other diseases that lupus can be misdiagnosed as include fibromyalgia, blood or tissue cancers, viral infections, multiple sclerosis, certain allergies, scleroderma, and rheumatoid arthritis. Leprosy, a bacterial infection, produces skin lesions that look like discoid lupus. Lyme disease, which is a bacterial infection transmitted by ticks, can look like lupus, and some lupus patients' blood tests are false positive for Lyme disease.

Another reason that lupus is often difficult to diagnose is that there is no single diagnostic test for the disease, and this can mean that the diverse symptoms may not be readily related to a single disease. The authors of *The Lupus Handbook for Women* explain, "Many women with lupus say that their complaints, at least initially, were dismissed by their physicians as unimportant. In some cases, vague symptoms such as fatigue or general achiness are quickly labeled psychosomatic [imagined]."[8]

A patient may have to consult several doctors before a diagnosis of lupus is made. Generally, a specialist known as a rheumatologist (a doctor who specializes in diseases involving inflammation) is the one to definitively diagnose and treat lupus. Because lupus can affect numerous parts of the body, other specialists may also be consulted to assess damages to

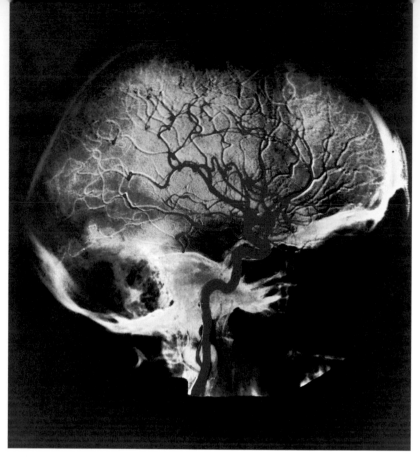

In this computer-enhanced photo of an angiogram, dye has been injected into the blood vessels of the brain. Tests like this can help to diagnose lupus.

organs—an ophthalmologist to assess damage to the eyes, a nephrologist to diagnose and treat kidney problems, a cardiologist for heart problems, a hematologist to deal with problems in the blood, and a neurologist for problems with the brain.

The Diagnostic Process

The diagnostic process begins with the physician taking a medical history of the patient. This includes a discussion of the person's symptoms, family history of certain diseases, past illnesses, past and current medications, exposure to toxic substances, and so on. Then the physician performs a physical examination, checking vital signs like pulse, blood pressure, and temperature along with an exam of the entire body. The doctor then orders appropriate laboratory tests in order to make an accurate diagnosis and to confirm any suspicions presented by the medical history and physical exam.

Typical blood tests performed include a complete blood count (CBC), which analyzes red blood cells, white blood cells, and platelets; most patients with lupus have an abnormal CBC, with lower than normal levels of red cells, white cells, and platelets. Other tests include a blood chemistry panel, which typically evaluates a variety of body functions such as blood sugar, kidney function, liver function, blood fats, and other body chemistry.

Additional tests performed on the patient's blood may include tests measuring inflammation and antibodies (substances produced by the immune system) to the self (lupus patients show antibodies to their own tissues). Antibody tests include the antinuclear antibody (ANA), anti-DNA, anti-sm, and antiphospholipid tests. The ANA test is used as a primary diagnostic tool for lupus, but sometimes a person with a positive ANA test may not have the disease. Other diseases that also show a positive ANA test include scleroderma, Sjogren's syndrome, rheumatoid arthritis, liver disease, mononucleosis, leprosy, thyroiditis, and multiple sclerosis. In addition, about 20 percent of healthy individuals will show a weakly positive ANA, which is not associated with any disease. People with DLE often have a negative ANA test but still have lupus, so the ANA cannot be used as a sole criterion for diagnosing lupus.

Sometimes a physician will order a skin biopsy to help confirm a diagnosis of lupus, particularly of DLE, which can mimic other skin conditions like rosacea and fungal infections. A lupus band test, which measures certain chemicals on a skin sample, may also be performed to help confirm a diagnosis of lupus.

A chest X-ray, lung scan, lung biopsy, and heart ultrasound may be used to assess lung and heart damage from lupus. Often fluid builds up in the lungs and must be measured to achieve an accurate diagnosis. An ECG, or electrocardiogram, can reveal heart problems related to lupus. It measures the

The Antinuclear Antibody (ANA) Test

The ANA laboratory test is the most sensitive diagnostic test for confirming a diagnosis of lupus when characteristic symptoms are also seen in a patient. This test is positive in 97 percent of individuals with lupus. However, a positive ANA test by itself, without symptoms of lupus, may not indicate that lupus is present because other diseases also involve a positive ANA.

ANA laboratory tests include a titer and a pattern. The titer indicates how many times a laboratory technician has to dilute plasma (the liquid portion of blood) to get a sample free of anti-nuclear antibodies. A titer of 1:640, for example, shows a greater concentration of antinuclear antibodies than one of 1:320. A titer of 1:80 is considered to be ANA positive. ANA titers may change during the course of a disease and do not necessarily indicate that the disease is more or less active.

The pattern seen on the ANA test may be smooth, speckled, peripheral, or nucleolar. Usually a speckled or peripheral pattern is found in patients with lupus, so the pattern, as well as the titer, can be used as an indication of the disease.

heart rate, rhythm, and size of the heart and indicates whether the lining of the heart or heart muscle are inflamed.

Various tests such as an angiogram, where dye is injected into the blood vessels of the brain so they can be studied by X-ray, or a spinal tap, where fluid is withdrawn from the spinal cord, may be done to help diagnose vasculitis of the central nervous system, an inflammation of the brain's blood vessels due to lupus. This complication can occur early in the course of the disease and can be fatal or lead to lasting mental effects.

Diagnostic Criteria

Because of the many symptoms and tests that can be used to diagnose lupus, the American College of Rheumatology has devised certain formal criteria for diagnosing the disease. In order for a diagnosis of lupus to be made, a patient must have at least four of eleven named criteria. The first group of criteria affect the skin and include sensitivity to the sun, mouth sores, a butterfly-shaped rash on the face (also known as a malar rash), and disk-shaped sores on the skin. The second group of criteria involves internal organs. These include arthritis (inflammation of the joints), serositis (inflammation of the lining of the lungs or heart), kidney disease, or disorders of the nervous system such as seizures or psychosis that have no other explanation. The third group of criteria is laboratory tests that show blood abnormalities such as too few red blood cells, white blood cells, or platelets, and blood tests that show certain kinds of antibodies such as ANA.

If a person has at least four of the eleven criteria, not necessarily all at the same time, they can be diagnosed with lupus. Once a diagnosis of lupus has been made, certain tests can be used as indicators that the disease has gotten worse. Even though tests can be used to track the progression of lupus, there is no way that a doctor can predict which patients will get worse and which ones will show a mild ongoing case of lupus. Some patients experience frequent flares, or worsening of symptoms, while others may go into remission for months or even years. According to the Lupus Foundation of America, "It is frequently said about lupus that the only thing that is predictable about lupus is its unpredictability."[9]

CHAPTER TWO

What Causes Lupus?

Like the symptoms and diagnosis of lupus, the causes of the disease are complex, as explained by experts at the Mayo Clinic in Rochester, Minnesota:

> Lupus is an autoimmune disease, which means that instead of just attacking foreign substances, such as bacteria and viruses, the immune system also turns against healthy tissue. This leads to inflammation and damage to various parts of the body, including the joints, skin, kidneys, heart, lungs, blood vessels and brain. Why autoimmune diseases occur still isn't well understood. But doctors believe that like many diseases, lupus results from a combination of factors, which may include heredity, environment and hormones.[10]

The immune system, when it is working properly, creates antibodies to fight foreign invaders like viruses and bacteria. But something goes wrong in the immune system of lupus patients. According to the author of *The Lupus Book*, it fails to recognize certain parts of the body as self and attacks them as if they were a foreign antigen:

> In other words, the normal surveillance system is altered in lupus, resulting in accelerated inflammatory responses and autoantibody formation: the autoantibodies in turn attack the body's own cells and tissues. It is as if our body's police force found itself unable to tolerate healthy, law-abiding cells and schemed to undermine them.[11]

Types of Autoantibodies

There are many types of autoantibodies that can produce symptoms of lupus. Lupus patients' blood generally shows several types that fall into four categories. The first category includes antibodies that form against materials in the nucleus, or center, of the cells. Examples are antinuclear antibody (ANA), the most widely known SLE antibody, and anti-DNA, also commonly seen in lupus. The second category is antibodies that form against the cell surface such an anti-Ro and anti-La, both commonly seen in lupus patients. The third category is antibodies to different types of cells such as red blood cells, white blood cells, platelets, nerve cells, or kidney cells. Here the antibody forms against the entire cell, not just the nucleus or cell surface. The fourth is antibodies that form against certain chemical compounds that circulate in the blood. An example would be antibodies to chemical compounds called rheumatoid factors.

Depending on which cells or organs these autoantibodies attack, different symptoms and signs of lupus are produced. For example, if the immune system attacks red blood cells, the result is anemia, a shortage of red blood cells. If kidney cells are targeted, kidney disease will result. Pericarditis, or inflammation of the sac around the heart, occurs when autoantibodies attack the pericardium. High blood cholesterol and high blood pressure, which make people with lupus more prone to heart attacks, can be caused by inflammation in the blood vessels that results from autoantibodies attacking these blood vessels. When inflammation occurs, clogged arteries can be stretched and torn, allowing blood clots to form. These clots can block the blood supply to the heart and lead to a heart attack. Usually patients prone to developing blood clots show what are called antiphospholipid antibodies in their blood.

Genes and Lupus

There are several factors that can cause the immune system to produce the autoantibodies that lead to lupus. One factor is genetics. Genes are the part of a DNA (deoxyribonucleic acid)

Polymerase Chain Reaction

Polymerase chain reaction is a technique commonly used by research scientists to analyze DNA samples. The procedure was developed in 1985 by chemist Kary Mullis, who received a Nobel Prize for his work. It is sometimes called DNA amplification because it entails replicating a DNA segment to produce a large sample that can be easily analyzed.

The technique begins by immersing DNA in a solution that contains the enzyme DNA polymerase, a series of DNA's chemical building blocks known as nucleotides, and primers that bind with the ends of a DNA segment. The solution is heated to break apart the DNA strands. When it cools the primers bind to the separated strands and the DNA polymerase builds new strands by joining the primers to the nucleotides. The process is repeated so that billions of copies of a small piece of DNA can be fabricated in several hours. This technique has been used to identify genes that make people susceptible to lupus.

molecule that transmits hereditary information from parents to their offspring. When a gene is damaged it results in a change called a mutation. Mutated genetic material can be passed from either the mother or the father to a child. Mutations can also result from damage to genes that occurs after a child is born. Either way the altered genetic instructions may cause various malfunctions, producing certain diseases or disorders.

Lupus is not directly inherited, but sufferers may be born with certain mutations that make them susceptible to developing it. Many patients have mutated genes that are in the class known as HLA (human leukocyte antigen) genes. These genes are found on chromosome six, which regulates the immune system. It appears that multiple gene defects in this class may make a person susceptible to developing lupus. Research has also shown that certain regions on chromosomes 1, 2, 4, and 16 contain genes that may also regulate susceptibility to lupus.

Scientists use two main types of methods in their search for specific genes and mutations that may influence a disease like lupus. One method is linkage studies, in which researchers look at particular regions of chromosomes to see if they are linked to lupus in families in which people have the disease. Generally, families with more than one member who is affected by lupus are used in these studies. The researchers take many small pieces of DNA from each chromosome in each family member. The scientists then increase the pieces of DNA in number using a technique called polymerase chain reaction (PCR). Then they compare the pieces of DNA from family members with lupus to those who do not have the disease. If a particular gene is involved in lupus, those people who have the disease should share that segment of the chromosome housing that particular gene.

When many families are evaluated in this way, it is possible for researchers to identify specific genes that can predispose an individual to lupus. Thus far investigators have found over one hundred genes that they think play a role in lupus susceptibility.

Another type of genetic study used to identify genes responsible for triggering lupus is called an association study. In this kind of research scientists look for mutations in genes that are thought to be involved in susceptibility to lupus. They then compare the frequency of the mutation in people with lupus to those without the disease. If the gene is indeed involved in lupus, it will be found more frequently in people with the disease compared to a control population. In this way individual genes in the region can be studied to see if they are associated with the disease.

The fact that researchers have found a genetic component to lupus susceptibility means that family members of people with the disease are at increased risk for developing it. Doctors estimate that this risk is 10 percent for daughters of lupus patients and 2 percent for sons. Identical twins, who have the

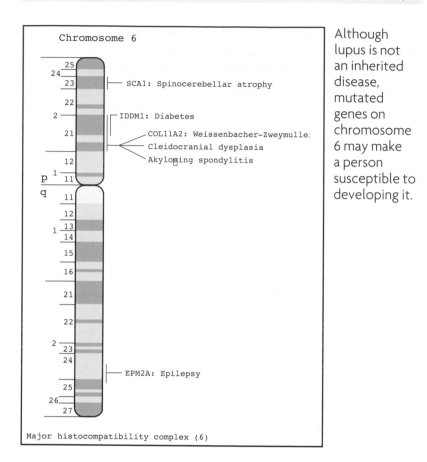

Chromosome 6

25
24
23   — SCA1: Spinocerebellar atrophy
22
2 —   ┌ IDDM1: Diabetes
21   COL11A2: Weissenbacher-Zweymulle:
              Cleidocranial dysplasia
12   Akyloging spondylitis
p 1   11
q   11
12
1 13
14
15
16
21
22
2   23
24
        — EPM2A: Epilepsy
25
26
27

Major histocompatibility complex (6)

Although lupus is not an inherited disease, mutated genes on chromosome 6 may make a person susceptible to developing it.

same genes, have a 26 to 70 percent chance of both having the disease, which indicates that certain genes play a big role in susceptibility to lupus. However, other factors besides genetics must also be involved since the chance of identical twins both having lupus is not 100 percent.

Environmental Factors

A genetic predisposition is only part of what causes lupus. There are also environmental factors that contribute to the disease and to making it worse in people who have a genetic susceptibility. Chemicals called aromatic amines have been linked to causing or aggravating lupus. These include hair dyes, tobacco smoke, and food colorings and preservatives.

People who metabolize these chemicals slowly may be prone to lupus, though only those who also have certain predisposing genes will actually develop the disease. Other chemicals like silicone, polyvinylchloride, trichloroethylene, and altered cooking oils have also been associated with lupus in persons who are genetically susceptible. Silicone is commonly used in adhesives, protective coatings, paints, electrical insulation, and synthetic rubber. Polyvinylchloride, also known as PVC, is a plastic used to make tubing, vinyl siding, and linoleum. Trichloroethylene is a colorless liquid used as a solvent to remove grease from metal parts and is also used in adhesives, paint removers, and spot removers. Altered cooking oils are oils that have been chemically refined to make them last longer and resist heat better. For example, extra virgin olive oil is unaltered, making it susceptible to heat damage and spoilage, whereas standard olive oil is refined, so it has a longer shelf life and tolerates high heat. Alfalfa sprouts can also cause or aggravate lupus in people with a genetic predisposition for the disease. Fish oil may also aggravate lupus but research findings on this have been contradictory.

Lupus patients and their families need to make careful choices with their diets, reading nutrition labels to avoid some kinds of additives and preservatives that exacerbate their symptoms.

Ultraviolet rays from the sun are an environmental factor proven to affect lupus. It appears that when ultraviolet radiation strikes the skin, it can damage DNA and result in the body producing anti-DNA antibodies that then lead to symptoms of lupus.

People who carry predisposing genes for lupus can also have the disease process started or worsened by a virus. Viruses linked to lupus include myxoviruses, reoviruses, Epstein Barr, and retroviruses. Myxoviruses cause colds, influenza, mumps, measles, and canine distemper. Reoviruses infect the human respiratory and digestive tracts, usually without disease symptoms, but sometimes causing diarrhea or upper respiratory infections. Retroviruses cause various types of cancer, as well as AIDS, which is caused by the retrovirus HIV. Studies show that people with lupus have elevated levels of antibodies to some of these viruses in their blood. Some experts believe that it is very likely that a virus or viruses that remain in the body after infection may turn out to be a primary cause of lupus. According to lupus expert Dr. Sheldon Blau:

> It is likely when the primary cause of lupus is found—and it will be found eventually—it will turn out to be a virus,

Exposure to certain chemicals, like the products made of polyvinyl chloride shown here, may cause lupus to develop in people who are susceptible or make it worse in those who already have it.

Drugs That Can Cause DILE*	
Name of Drug	**Used to Treat**
D-penicillamine	rheumatoid arthritis
hydralazine	high blood pressure
isoniazid	tuberculosis
phenytoin	epilepsy
procainamide	abnormal heart rhythm
quinidine	abnormal heart rhythm

*Dozens of other drugs have been known to cause DILE. However, 90% of DILE cases are due to side effects resulting from the above six drugs.

Source: MedicineNet.com. Available online at: http://www.medicinenet.com/systemic_lupus/article.htm

whether a retrovirus, a herpes virus, or some other type that behaves in an unusual manner (or is permitted to behave in an unusual manner in some individuals, perhaps those with particular genetic characteristics).[12]

Some researchers have found that lupus patients' dogs had higher than normal levels of autoantibodies characteristic of lupus. This finding has led scientists to ask whether the patients or the dogs could be transmitting antibodies to each other. The answer, however, is unknown, since lupus has never been found to be a contagious disease. Just because human lupus sufferers and their pets have higher than normal autoantibodies does not mean one is causing the condition in the other. The link between dogs and humans found in some research studies may just be a coincidence, or there may be a connection that researchers do not yet understand.

Drugs and Lupus

Certain drugs are also known to cause or aggravate lupus in people with a genetic predisposition. Over seventy different

Many people find the deep breathing, stretching and strengthening exercises of yoga to be beneficial in reducing stress and enhancing physical health.

drugs have this effect. Most cause problems by making the person extra sensitive to the sun or by promoting an allergy-like reaction. Some antibiotics used to fight bacterial infections are notorious for worsening lupus symptoms. Sulfa-based antibiotics are most likely to do this. Susan, for example, had SLE and developed a bladder infection. Her doctor prescribed Bactrim, a sulfa-based antibiotic, and soon she showed a bright red rash on her face, arms, and neck, along with swollen wrists and knees and a temperature of 102 degrees. Blood tests showed that her red and white blood cell counts were also diminished. The doctor had to take her off Bactrim and prescribe a different type of antibiotic.

Nonsteroidal anti-inflammatory drugs (NSAIDs) like ibuprofen are also known to worsen lupus in some patients. Brand names of ibuprofen are Advil or Motrin. Many doctors do not prescribe these drugs for lupus patients for this reason, though some do recommend them because they help alleviate symptoms for a lot of people with lupus.

Drugs that actually cause the type of lupus known as drug induced lupus erythematosus (DILE) are hydralazine, a treatment for high blood pressure; procainamide, used to treat abnormal heart rhythms; methyldopa, taken for high blood pressure; isoniazid, a treatment for tuberculosis; chlorpromazine, used to treat some mental disorders; TNF blockers, a type of arthritis medication; and D-penicillamine, used to treat arthritis, lead poisoning, or Wilson's disease. DILE is reversible; once the patient stops taking the offending drug, the lupus disappears within a few months.

Researchers believe that some of the ways that drugs cause DILE are similar to the ways that other types of lupus like SLE are caused. The drugs can bind to a part of a cell that alters DNA, causing the person's immune system to manufacture anti-DNA antibodies. Or the drug may activate T or B lymphocytes that are involved in making antibodies to other body tissues. Sometimes certain drugs break down into chemicals that promote the formation of autoantibodies. Genetic factors can also contribute to DILE—for example, people who are genetically predisposed to metabolize certain drugs slowly are prone to develop DILE when given these drugs.

Stress and Lupus

Another environmental factor that can cause or worsen lupus is stress. Emotional stress can induce a flare-up of the disease

Stress can cause lupus flare-ups, but biofeedback machines can help patients keep their stress under control.

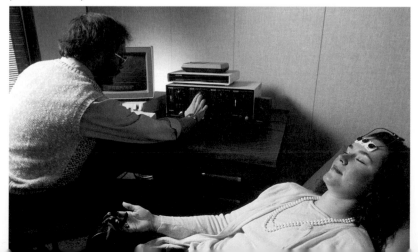

in patients who have it and sometimes can trigger the disorder in people with a genetic predisposition. Tiffany, for example, developed lupus shortly after the death of her father. As she explained:

> My doctor told me that stress is definitely linked to lupus. High levels for a long time, or stress that isn't channeled properly can spark autoimmune diseases and can flare up lupus…. My father was a healthy man who died without warning from a heart attack in January…. The funeral was in early February, but we couldn't bury him until May when the snow was gone and the ground thawed. This really dragged things out and I couldn't find closure for so long. Between his death and his burial, I was back at work trying to keep up in this very hectic and fast-paced career in advertising. That just added to the stress, and then I got engaged (which is a good thing, but still stressful!)…. That June I felt the first symptoms of lupus when I got swollen fingers and painful wrist joints. I went to the doctor in July and he was very quick to take blood tests for lupus and Lyme disease and he told me right away that I had lupus. I'm not sure if stress was the sole trigger for my lupus, but it seems obvious to me that the two are connected. So much was going on in my life at that time.[13]

Lupus and Hormones

Hormones can also play a role in causing lupus. The fact that about 90 percent of lupus patients are women suggests that female hormones have a great deal to do with the disease.

Hormones are chemical messengers produced by certain organs in the body. The female reproductive organs produce hormones called estrogen and progesterone. Male hormones produced by male reproductive organs are called androgens; the most important of these is testosterone. Estrogen can provoke lupus by causing an autoimmune reaction. For example, many women with lupus have an increase in symptoms before

The Most Common Causes of Death in Lupus Patients

The most common causes of death in lupus patients are heart disease, kidney failure, and infections. The heart and kidney disease result from the autoimmune process, while infections usually come from a decreased ability of the body to fight foreign invaders due to treatments that reduce the immune response.

The autoimmune attack on the heart and circulatory system can lead to the following conditions, which, in turn, place the patient at great risk for heart attack and death:

- Plaque buildup in the arteries
- Stiffness in the arteries
- High cholesterol levels
- High blood pressure
- Congestive heart failure, where the heart can no longer pump enough blood to the rest of the body
- Pericarditis, an inflammation of the sac surrounding the heart
- Blood clots

The body's attack on kidney cells damage the glomeruli, or filtering units in the kidneys. Once this happens the kidneys can no longer filter wastes from the blood, and these wastes can build up and result in death. Kidney failure can be manifested in the following ways:

- Large amounts of protein in the urine
- Blood in the urine
- Low blood protein
- Swelling in the hands or ankles

Many lupus patients suffer from high cholesterol and high blood pressure which can cause blood clots (pictured) to form and lead to heart attacks.

menstrual periods or when using birth control pills, when estrogen levels are high. Androgens, on the other hand, tend to suppress autoimmunity, and males with lupus tend to have lower than normal levels of androgens.

A Variety of Causes

Whether it is hormones, stress, drugs, or other causes, all of these factors work in a similar way. They all provoke the immune system to produce antibodies against the self in a genetically predisposed person. Knowing about the mechanisms behind the various causes of lupus can in turn lead doctors to treat the disease with medications that inhibit this autoimmune response.

CHAPTER THREE

How Is Lupus Treated?

Although there is no cure for lupus, certain medications and other treatments can effectively control the disease in many patients. As stated by the Lupus Foundation of America:

> For most people with lupus, effective treatment can minimize symptoms, reduce inflammation and pain, help maintain normal functions, and stop the development of serious complications. Just as the symptoms of lupus may vary from one individual to another, its treatment is tailored to the different specific problems that arise in each person.[14]

Sometimes it takes months or even years before a physician finds the right combination of drugs and other therapies to control an individual's lupus. Even in a patient whose disease is under control, the person may still experience flares, where symptoms become worse. Warning signs of a flare include increased fatigue, new or higher fever, increased pain, development or worsening of a rash, swollen joints, or other new symptoms. When a flare occurs, the physician must be notified immediately and he or she may have to change the patient's medications.

Philip Hench

When Dr. Philip Hench used the newly discovered chemical cortisone to successfully treat arthritic patients in 1949, it revolutionized the treatment of other autoimmune diseases such as lupus. Hench was born in 1896 in Pittsburgh, Pennsylvania. He graduated from Lafayette College in Easton, Pennsylvania, in 1916, and then he enlisted in the medical corps of the United States Army in 1917. He was transferred to the reserve corps and completed his medical training at the University of Pittsburgh, receiving a doctorate in medicine in 1920.

Hench went on to study at the Mayo Clinic in Minnesota and at Freiberg University and the von Müller Clinic in Munich, Germany, before taking a position as a professor of medicine at the Mayo Foundation. From 1942 to 1946 he served in the Army's Medical Corps, becoming chief of the medical service and director of the army's Rheumatism Center at the Army and Navy General Hospital.

Back at the Mayo Clinic after World War II, Hench continued to specialize in arthritic diseases. He collaborated on studies with Dr. E.C. Kendall, who isolated several steroids from the adrenal gland in people. Convinced that the steroid called Compound E (later called cortisone) could help alleviate pain in people with arthritis, Hench tried the drug on patients with positive results. As well as receiving the Nobel Prize in 1950 for his efforts, Hench was also awarded many awards in rheumatology. He died in March 1965.

Dr. Philip Hench discovered that the chemical cortisone could successfully treat arthritis and other autoimmune diseases such as lupus. He won the Nobel Prize in 1950.

Disease Modifying Drugs

Prior to the late 1940s, the only semi-effective treatments for lupus were aspirin and skin salves. Then in 1949 Dr. Philip Hench of the Mayo Clinic in Minnesota showed that the newly discovered hormone cortisone could effectively treat rheumatoid arthritis, another autoimmune disorder. Doctors began using cortisone to treat lupus, often with life-saving results.

Later other researchers showed that two other types of drugs, antimalarials and immune suppressives, could also be used to effectively treat lupus. These two classes of drugs, along with cortisone, remain the primary medications used to modify the course of lupus today.

Steroids

The most commonly used lupus disease modifying drugs are the steroid cortisone and its derivatives. While steroids can save the lives of lupus patients, they must be used carefully, as they can be dangerous. As the author of *The Lupus Book* explains:

> Steroids are the most effective and most misunderstood treatment for lupus. They are also the most used and abused therapeutic interventions for the disease. Simply stated, if organ-threatening disease is present and steroids are not prescribed, the patient usually loses function in that organ. If mild disease activity is present, other therapeutic alternatives with or without steroids are available, but many physicians have little experience in using these alternatives and tend to overuse steroids.[15]

Steroids are hormones made by the adrenal glands above the kidneys. They decrease inflammation and decrease the number of circulating lymphocytes—the white blood cells responsible for remembering immune responses. Synthetic steroids can be administered to decrease the activity of the immune system.

These include cortisone, prednisone, dexamethasone, and others. Prednisone is most frequently used to treat lupus.

Steroids are usually given orally. There are also topical steroid creams and ointments that can be used for skin rashes and lesions. Sometimes doctors inject steroids into discoid lesions, and sometimes steroids are given intravenously to critically ill patients who are in the hospital. They can also be injected into a joint or muscle to alleviate inflammation.

Patients with active, organ-threatening lupus are usually managed on daily high doses of steroids. Those with severe flare-ups of non-organ-threatening lupus are usually given moderate daily doses, and patients with mild non-organ-threatening lupus are given low daily doses. Some patients only need to be on steroids during active disease flare-ups; then the dosage is gradually tapered off as symptoms improve.

Without steroids, many lupus patients with severe disease would die quickly. Unfortunately, these drugs have undesirable

Steroids are usually given orally, but some can be injected into joints, or even given intravenously for critically ill patients.

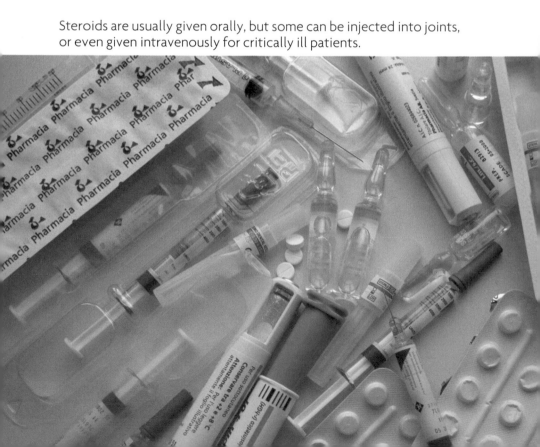

side effects, so taking them is a double-edged sword. They can cause agitation, rapid heart rate, sleeplessness, and heartburn. The skin gradually becomes thin and wrinkles easily from steroids. Bruises appear, hair loss on the head is common, facial hair increases, and acne develops. Wound healing is impaired. Muscle weakness and loss of calcium in the bones occurs. The loss of calcium may lead to osteoporosis, or thinning bones that break easily. Diabetes is common from long-term steroid use, as is weight gain. Blood fats like cholesterol increase. Cataracts and glaucoma, which can cause blindness, may develop in the eyes. Steroids thin intestinal walls and may lead to holes in these walls. The risk of infection of all types is greater because steroids prevent antibodies from killing bacteria, viruses, fungi, and parasites.

Not all of these side effects occur in everyone who takes steroids, but they are more likely in those who take high doses for a long time. Most patients on steroids must also take medications to protect the gastrointestinal system from ulcers, calcium to protect bones, and sedatives to sleep. They must follow a low sodium, low fat diet to help prevent heart disease.

Doctors try to keep patients on as low a dose of steroids as possible to prevent side effects. However, when going from high to lower doses, the dosage must be tapered gradually to give the body a chance to begin making natural steroids again; when synthetic steroids are taken, the body stops making its own.

Antimalarials

Malaria is a severe disease transmitted by mosquitoes and marked by fevers. Quinine and related compounds are known to prevent and cure malaria. Since these drugs also have anti-inflammatory and anti-infection properties, they can be useful in treating lupus. In fact, during World War II, when soldiers were given Atabrine, a synthetic form of quinine, to prevent malaria, this drug improved symptoms in men with rheumatoid arthritis or lupus. Atabrine is no longer manufactured, but

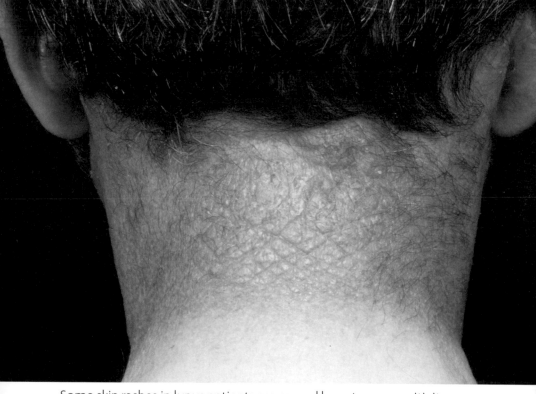

Some skin rashes in lupus patients are caused by extreme sensitivity to the sun. Antimalarial drugs can reduce the damage to exposed skin.

other antimalarials such as hydroxychloroquine, also known as Plaquenil, are still used today as treatments for lupus.

Antimalarials help keep ultraviolet light from damaging skin, thereby diminishing skin rashes. They also help with discoid lesions, mouth sores, hair loss, swollen and aching joints, inflammation of the lining of the lungs and heart, cognitive dysfunction, and fatigue. Given early in the course of lupus, they lead to fewer disease flare-ups and prevent organ-threatening complications. Many lupus patients take Plaquenil for at least two years. Some are able to discontinue the drug, while others must continue to use it indefinitely. This drug can have side effects of a rash, aching, nervousness, headache, nausea, and blurred vision.

Immunosuppressives

The third class of drugs used to treat lupus is immunosuppressives, also known as cytotoxic or chemotherapy drugs. These are used when the patient has severe organ-threatening lupus and steroids alone are not sufficient, or when the patient cannot tolerate high doses of steroids. Lupus expert Dr. Robert Katz explains how these drugs work:

> Cells in the body divide and grow at varying rates. Examples of rapidly dividing cells include the antibody-producing cells of the immune system, blood cells, hair cells, gonadal cells, and malignant cells. Cytotoxic (cyto means cell, toxic means damage) drugs work by targeting and damaging the cells that grow at a rapid rate. In lupus the immune system is hyperactive and produces autoantibodies at a rapid rate of growth. Cytotoxic medicines have their greatest effect against rapidly dividing cells and, therefore, can be beneficial in the treatment of lupus by suppressing activity.[16]

A drug called Cytoxan is frequently given to lupus patients intravenously once a month to treat severe disease. Unfortunately it can cause severe nausea, hair loss, sterility, and cancer. Other drugs like azathioprine and methotrexate are also used to decrease inflammation, but they too have numerous serious side effects. Other drugs like Cyclosporin A, CellCept, and Avara, which are used primarily to suppress the immune system in organ transplant patients, are also used to treat lupus. These can make a patient very susceptible to infections of all kinds, as they inhibit the activity of the entire immune system.

Other Medications

Besides the primary disease modifying medications used to treat lupus, many patients also need other drugs to deal with specific problems. People who experience severe fatigue, for example, may require iron, thyroid, modafinil, or other medicines.

The anemia that frequently accompanies lupus may have to be treated according to its cause. If the anemia is caused by inflammation, prednisone may be sufficient to deal with the problem. If it is due to an iron deficiency, iron pills may be prescribed. If kidney disease or chemotherapy drugs are causing the anemia,

the drugs erythropoietin or darbepoietin may be given to stimulate the bone marrow to make more red blood cells.

Many lupus patients must take anti-inflammatory medications such as aspirin or other nonsteroidal anti-inflammatory
drugs (NSAIDS) in addition to the steroids given for pain and
inflammation. Aspirin lowers fever, diminishes joint and muscle aches and inflammation, and decreases inflammation of the
sacs of the heart and lungs. It has no affect on the skin, kidneys,
nervous system, or blood problems common in the disease, nor
does it put lupus into remission.

Too much aspirin can irritate the stomach or cause ringing
in the ears, so it must be used sparingly. Other NSAIDS, including naproxen, ibuprofen, and others are more potent than
aspirin in relieving pain and inflammation but have more side
effects. They can damage the stomach with ulcers and cause
serious kidney and liver damage. They can also induce lupus
flares in some patients. Despite these dangers, approximately
80 percent of all lupus patients take NSAIDS on a regular or
intermittent basis, as it allows them to function better. Doctors
emphasize that lupus sufferers should take these drugs under a
doctor's supervision even though they can be purchased without a prescription, and that frequent blood tests to monitor kidney and liver function are performed. Medications that protect
the stomach from ulcers should also be taken with NSAIDS.

Some doctors prescribe a male hormone called DHEA to
treat symptoms of cognitive dysfunction and fatigue. Some
patients benefit from danazol, an anti-estrogen drug that can
improve low red blood cell and low platelet counts. Rashes
and skin lesions in lupus are sometimes treated with anti-acne
drugs like Accutane or with antileprosy medications like Dap-
sone or thalidomide.

Lupus and Depression

Because many lupus patients experience depression related
to having a chronic illness and from physical changes in the
nervous system, medication and other treatments for depression must often be prescribed. Severe cases of depression can

Some lupus patients visit psychotherapists to help them cope with feelings of depression.

be treated with a variety of antidepressant medications and/or tranquilizers, anti-anxiety agents, or sedatives. It is important that the medicines prescribed not interact adversely with any other medications the patient is taking. Sometimes medication for depression is prescribed by the person's lupus doctor; other times the patient may go to a psychiatrist who orders these drugs.

Along with medication, many physicians recommend that people who are depressed go for some sort of psychological therapy to help them deal with the negative thoughts and behaviors that are contributing to or resulting from the depression. Many therapists use cognitive behavioral therapy to help patients deal with depression and other emotional issues that come with having a chronic illness. This type of therapy aims to give the patient control over their negative thoughts and behaviors and turn them into more positive entities. For example, rather than thinking that lupus has ruined their life, patients can learn to replace this thought with the belief that even though lupus keeps them from doing certain things, it is a part of their life that they have to accept.

There are also other forms of psychotherapy that can be useful in the treatment of depression. In an article on the Lupus Canada web site a lupus patient shares with fellow lupus sufferers his positive experience with psychotherapy, despite initial misgivings about going for help:

> What I have learned through therapy and the right books being given to me to read at the right time has helped me learn that bad thinking CAN make feeling bad worse. Educating myself here has enabled me to better deal with the pains and losses associated with being sick. My pain levels haven't changed but the way I think, deal and live with the pain has changed immensely. Now I recommend seeing a psychologist to anyone. What possible harm could come by talking about what's bothering you or what your fears are except actually having to deal with them head on.[17]

Other Types of Lupus Treatments

Many lupus patients require other types of therapy in addition to drugs and psychotherapy, depending on specific problems associated with the disease. Rehabilitation therapy is common for people who have chronically inflamed joints and other discomfort. Physical and occupational therapists perform rehabilitation therapy. Physical therapists help the patient move inflamed joints without damaging them, teach the patient to improve conditioning, and give massages and other helpful treatments like applying hot packs where needed to soothe aching joints. Occupational therapists assist with activities of daily living by recommending devices such as splints, leg braces, special eating utensils if the hand joints are sore, and so on.

Lupus sufferers must also take measures to avoid sunlight, as ultraviolet radiation often triggers symptoms of rashes, achy joints, and fatigue. Wearing a sunscreen lotion helps protect

Lupus patients with kidney disease must undergo dialysis. A machine does the job of the kidney, cleaning the blood by removing fluids, minerals, and wastes.

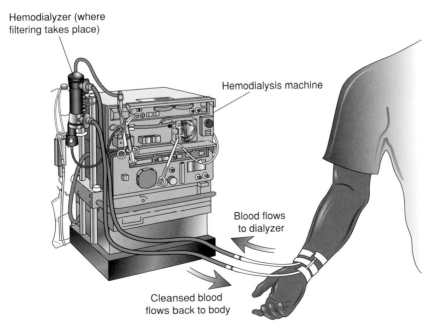

Hemodialyzer (where filtering takes place)

Hemodialysis machine

Blood flows to dialyzer

Cleansed blood flows back to body

against sunburn and harmful lupus symptoms, and physicians also recommend that lupus patients avoid being outside during peak sunlight hours of ten a.m. to three p.m. when the sun's rays are strongest. Many patients wear protective clothing that covers their whole body as well. Indoor fluorescent lights can also cause lupus flares, so doctors advise putting covers on this type of bulb.

Another element of lupus treatment is exercise. According to the author of *The Lupus Book*, "[Sensible] exercise is a very important part of managing lupus. It can strengthen muscles, improve flexibility, and promote a sense of well-being. Inactivity can promote osteoporosis, muscle weakness, and wasting. Patients who are not fit are less able to respond to various stresses in the environment."[18] Doctors recommend doing exercise that strengthens muscles and builds endurance without damaging joints. These include stretching, walking, swimming, and bicycling. If a joint or muscle is painful, experts say it is best not to exercise it, but rather to apply moist heat as in a bath or hot tub.

Patients with severe kidney disease from lupus must undergo a treatment called dialysis. The kidneys normally remove excess fluids, minerals, and wastes from the blood, a job that is essential to keeping us alive. Dialysis involves using a machine to do the same job. The most common method of kidney dialysis is called hemodialysis. The procedure involves hooking the patient up to a dialysis machine with an intravenous (IV) line and allowing the person's blood to flow through a tube to a special filter a few ounces at a time. The clean blood is then returned to the body through a second tube. The procedure takes three to five hours at a time and patients must undergo it three times per week. A second method called peritoneal dialysis is sometimes used for patients whose kidneys fail. Here, a soft tube similar to a feeding tube is inserted into the abdomen and a cleaning liquid called dialysis solution is run through the tube. The walls of the abdominal cavity are lined with a membrane called the peritoneum. This membrane allows waste products and extra fluid to pass from the blood into the dialysis solution, which is then drained from the body. This procedure must be done four times per day, and the solution must be left in the abdominal cavity for four to six hours each time. Many patients can perform peritoneal dialysis on their own and do not need to go to a hospital for it.

Alternative Treatments

All of the treatments described so far are the most traditional and common treatments prescribed by doctors of medicine. Since some of these treatments may not work or have unpleasant side effects, some patients try what are called alternative therapies to bring relief. Doctors caution that any alternative therapies that practitioners claim are miracle cures should be avoided because there is as yet no cure for lupus. Patients who try untested therapies and stop prescribed treatments may also do themselves great harm. It is important for patients to research any therapy they wish to try, making sure it is administered by a licensed practitioner, and also asking their primary care physician if the therapy is safe.

One type of alternative therapy that often helps lupus patients is acupuncture. This is a traditional Chinese healing technique that attempts to balance the life energy, or *chi*, by using fine needles inserted at specific sites on the skin. It has been proven to stimulate the release of endorphins (the body's natural pain killers) and other chemicals that diminish pain, so it is often used to treat the aches and pains of lupus. Some acu-

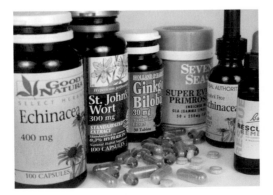

Herbs, like those pictured, may help relieve some symptoms of lupus, but should be used with extreme caution as they may interact negatively with prescribed medications.

Acupuncture

Many lupus patients find relief from pain through the alternative medical practice of acupuncture, which has been used in China since about 1600 b.c. Acupuncture gained attention in the United States in 1972, after then-president Richard Nixon traveled to China. During the trip a reporter traveling with Nixon became ill and required surgery. The Chinese doctors performed the surgery using only acupuncture as anesthesia, and this so impressed Nixon that he helped to organize a cultural exchange of medical doctors between the United States and China.

Today there are many licensed acupuncturists in the United States. These practitioners diagnose illness by asking the patient questions, by taking pulses at several points along the wrist, and by looking at the tongue. Then the acupuncturist inserts very fine needles into selected points on the skin that have been found to correspond to certain internal organs and conditions. The points on the skin are not necessarily located next to the internal organ they correspond to; for example, an acupuncture point on the leg may be used to treat a disease of the stomach. When certain acupuncture points are stimulated, this can lead to healing of diseases or relief of pain.

puncturists also prescribe herbs for their patients, but lupus doctors say that some herbs can interact adversely with prescription medicines and should not be used unless the lupus doctor approves it. Herbs are not regulated by the Food and Drug Administration (FDA) like drugs are, so sometimes it is difficult to assess what is being sold for what purpose.

Other herbs available in drug stores and health food stores have also been touted as helpful in lupus patients. A combination of the herbs frankincense, ginger, turmeric, and ashwa-

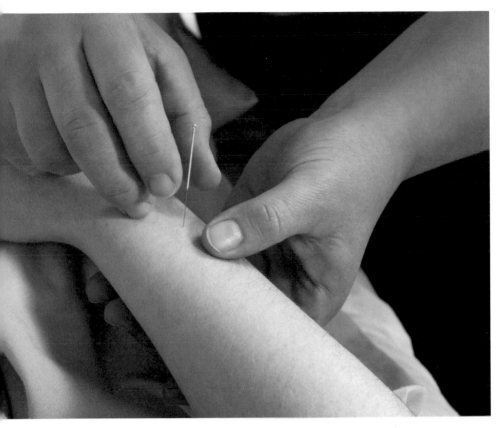

Acupuncture involves inserting fine needles at specific points on the body. These needles stimulate chemicals called endorphins that help reduce pain.

gandha can diminish inflammation and pain and seems safe to use. The herb St. John's wort may help relieve depression, and ginkgo may improve cognitive dysfunction. However, ginkgo can increase the effects of blood thinning medications used by patients with heart disease, so it must be used with caution. Feverfew has been touted for its ability to relieve pain, but lupus doctors say it cannot be used with any other pain medicines or with blood thinning medications because it can increase the effects of these drugs. Echinacea, an herb that is supposed to boost the immune system, should also be avoided by people with lupus because it can counteract the effects of steroids and immune suppressives and can also worsen liver damage caused by these drugs.

Chiropractic and craniosacral therapy, two additional forms of alternative healing, involve manipulation of the spine (in the case of chiropractic) and of the skull, spine, and fluid that flows around the brain and spinal cord (craniosacral therapy). Such treatments sometimes alleviate the pain involved in lupus, but no scientific studies have proven a definite positive effect. Most patients do not experience adverse effects from these treatments, so doctors say they are okay to try as long as the practitioners are licensed and experienced.

Magnet therapy refers to the use of magnetic strips attached to the body with tape or held against the body with a belt or mattress pad. Magnets have been used in healing for over two thousand years. In modern times they have become popular among athletes for treating sports-related injuries and have also been studied in people with various diseases. One 1997 study at the Baylor College of Medicine and the Institute for Rehabilitation and Research in Texas found that magnets relieved pain in patients experiencing post-polio syndrome, a condition that produces pain in the joints and muscles. Some lupus patients who have tried magnet therapy have also found pain relief, and since the treatment appears to be without side effects, experts say it is not dangerous even though it has not yet been scientifically proven to be helpful for lupus.

A variety of relaxation and stress reduction techniques have also been found to help some lupus patients cope with pain and anxiety associated with the disease. One method called biofeedback involves a person learning to control their body's responses such as heart rate and breathing to minimize stress and pain. Deep breathing exercises are another technique that can reduce pain and anxiety. Yoga is a series of exercises that combines deep breathing with specific postures to enhance mental and physical relaxation. Transcendental meditation teaches a person to focus on thoughts or objects to create an inner calm. T'ai chi is a series of slow, deliberate movements that contribute to physical and mental relaxation.

Lupus experts emphasize that any of these alternative therapies should be used in conjunction with, rather than instead of, conventional treatments. Otherwise, the patient risks dangerous complications that can be life threatening.

CHAPTER FOUR

Living With Lupus

Living with lupus is challenging and disturbing from the moment of diagnosis. Many patients feel frightened, angry, depressed, or even guilty when they receive the diagnosis. Some feel relieved because the diagnosis lets them know what is really wrong and that they are not just imagining their symptoms. But all in all, a diagnosis of lupus heralds a life that will change significantly. According to the authors of *The Lupus Handbook for Women*:

> Being diagnosed with lupus can be an overwhelming experience for a patient and her family. It's not easy to accept the fact that you or your loved one may have a chronic illness, particularly one that does not follow any predictable course. Lupus is synonymous with unpredictability. Even if you have mild disease, as most lupus patients do, you will still be living with the threat of a flare. And although you will probably be able to live a reasonable normal life, you may be limited in certain ways that you would not be if you did not have lupus. All of this can be very hard to swallow, particularly for the typical lupus patient—a young woman—who is just beginning her life as an adult.[19]

Men with lupus face similar coping issues. The emotional and physical adjustments that must be made are difficult for people of both sexes, and these changes are especially difficult

56

Children and teens with lupus may suffer emotional stress and face social problems that cause depression and anxiety.

Support Groups and Lupus

Many lupus patients find that support groups are very helpful, even if they are initially hesitant to join one. As stated in an article on the Lupus Foundation of America website:

> Support groups provide SLE patients with a confidential and comforting environment. They have the opportunity to share personal experiences, obtain useful information, and listen to the ideas and advice of those in similar situations. The meeting room is a place where emotional catharsis is encouraged; where no one is judged, accused, or disbelieved because their disease is "unseen," where true empathy is the norm rather than the exception ... Despite the fact that support groups provide numerous benefits, it is often difficult to dispel the myths that surround them—that meeting rooms are filled with melodramatic "victims" of disease, or that the act of listening to someone else's symptoms will make one's own problems worsen. To the contrary, many patients find that this type of organized, unconditional support can serve as a vital resource and healing tool, both in the short and long term.

Originally published in Darlene A. Croce, "The Importance of Support Groups for the SLE Patient," SLE in Clinical Practice, June 1999, Vol. 2, Issue 2. Reprinted on Lupus Foundation of America, www.lupus.org/education/topics/supportgroups.html

because family members and spouses may not understand that the lupus patient is really sick. Even when others do understand, patients may turn to lupus support groups for encouragement and information from others with the disease. "Even when family and friends are patient and encouraging, support groups can provide that understanding nod that a person who does not have lupus could never offer," says the author of *New Hope for People with Lupus*.[20] Patients can find support groups through physicians, hospitals, or the Internet. Some groups have meetings with speakers and informal discussions; others consist of online support networks where members correspond via the Internet.

Family Adjustments

Some lupus patients are faced with family members who resent the fact that the person can no longer keep up with household chores, workplace demands, or care of children. In fact, nearly half of all married women who develop lupus are divorced within five years for these reasons.

Even in cases that do not involve divorce, problems are frequent, as explained by one woman with lupus:

> Before I got sick, I did everything. I did the yard work, I ran the household, and I also worked. I had a lot of energy back then. When I was first diagnosed, my husband did help out a lot. But now he doesn't. I'm not sick every day, but there are days that I just can't even put the laundry in the machine or clear the dishes out of the sink. He waits for me to do it no matter what. When I try to talk about lupus, he won't listen. My husband just can't accept the fact that I'm sick or that this is something that may last forever.[21]

Some patients have the opposite problem—that a spouse or parent tries to keep them from doing anything at all because of the illness. This requires the patient to assert herself and let others know that she can lead a fairly normal life except for when she has flares in the lupus. Experts also recommend that people with lupus try to live as full a life as possible, focusing on people and things other than their illness. But when experiencing an active flare or when fatigue from the disease sets in, a patient should not hesitate to ask loved ones for help in managing chores, child care, and other tasks.

Some patients are lucky enough to have family members or friends to offer physical and emotional support when needed. Kim, for example, was diagnosed with lupus at age seventeen and relied on her mother for support:

> Having lupus can be very scary and very lonely if you have to go through it by yourself. There were times when I couldn't go out with my friends because of my fatigue and I just couldn't do everything that they could do. This was really tough to face in high school. If I didn't have my mom to fall back on, I don't know how I could stand it. She was my friend at home who was always there. I think it's important to have someone like that—a friend, an aunt, a mom or dad, anyone—because it's hard to go through this without someone to pick you up when you're down or just to give you a shoulder to cry on. I know I need emotional support, and, fortunately, I have it.[22]

Kids and Teens with Lupus

Having lupus can be stressful for teens who are especially concerned about appearing different from their peers and who may not take prescribed medications because of side effects like a swollen face from prednisone. Joelle, for example, liked to go to the beach with her friends and stayed out late at night. The sun exposure worsened her rash, she became very fatigued, and her joints became swollen and painful. She would not take her prescribed prednisone until her anemia became so severe that she had to be hospitalized. Then, after extensive talks with her doctors about the importance of properly treating her lupus, she began taking better care of herself.

Consistently applying special sunscreens is important for lupus patients who have extreme sensitivity to the sun's rays.

Teens are also typically inclined to assert their independence from their parents. As Robert H. Phillips, PhD, explains:

> The natural inclination of any parent is to become over-protective when a child is sick.... In all likelihood, this will increase adolescent rebellion. Rebellion is a normal part of adolescence, regardless of whether or not lupus

is involved. Parents should try not to be overprotective, and should try to be as tolerant and as understanding as they can.[23]

Children as well as teens with lupus may also experience social and emotional upheavals because of the disease. As Dr. Jimmy Lawrence of the Nemours Children's Clinic in Pensacola, Florida, explains:

> Even when the condition is stabilized, these children are condemned to daily medications, ongoing doctor visits, and medical testing. They are aware that they are different from their siblings and friends; they are often in pain and they experience negative side effects from their medications, and they know their parents are worried.[24]

Lupus may interfere with school and friendships for kids and teens, since flares may mean that they cannot go to school for awhile or cannot socialize with their friends if they are too sick. Scott, a twelve year old with lupus, writes in his book *Loopy Lupus Helps Tell Scott's Story* about how lupus changed his life and a little about how he was diagnosed:

> When I was little, I seemed to be just fine. But one day I came home from school and everything was different. My knees and ankles hurt. I had trouble running and playing with my friends. I was tired and couldn't do my homework because I just didn't feel well. I had a fever and I ached all over. Mom took me to the doctor's office. She and the doctors knew right away that I was sick, but they didn't know what was wrong until they did some special tests.[25]

Scott learned that lupus would impact his life every day, sometimes restricting his ability to play and learn. For other teens and kids with lupus, different aspects of lifestyle restrictions bother them more than others. Andy, 15, for example, said that "The worst part of lupus is the sun factor. I can't ski, play golf, tennis, or baseball; or go fishing without putting on sunscreen. Plus I have to wear special SPF-65 sunscreen with zinc oxide and put on my SPF-rated swim shirt before I even go into the pool."[26]

But kids and teens with lupus can make adjustments and still enjoy life with the right attitude, as Marissa, 11, said, "I played soccer, but there was too much running. So now I've switched to basketball—and I take lots of breaks. That way, my legs don't get so tired. At first a kid might think, 'oh, poor me.' But you can't think that way—you just have to think good thoughts."[27]

Lupus and Childbearing

Just as lupus poses special challenges for children and teenagers who have it, patients of different ages face other unique challenges because of the disease. The group most often affected by lupus is women of childbearing age. For them questions arise as to whether they can safely have babies. Until twenty-five years ago, most women with lupus who became pregnant either had a miscarriage (lost the baby before it could survive outside the womb) or a stillborn baby. But today doctors better understand lupus and its risks, and in many cases it is possible for lupus patients to have normal, healthy children.

Doctors say that a woman who decides to become pregnant should have her lupus under good control and should take a minimal amount of medications because drugs can cross the placenta and affect the fetus. Steroids seem to be safe to take during pregnancy, but antimalarials, chemotherapy drugs, and anti-inflammatory drugs are not. Women with severe organ-threatening disease or who are taking chemotherapy drugs are advised not to get pregnant since they have a high risk of having a fetus die and of having maternal organ failure.

Some women with mild or moderate lupus experience flare-ups of the disease if they become pregnant, while others find that pregnancy has no effect on or actually improves their lupus symptoms. Possible risks during pregnancy include preeclampsia, a condition that occurs when pregnant women experience kidney problems, which results in a dangerous rise in the mother's blood pressure, the presence of protein in the urine, and fluid retention that causes puffy ankles, fingers, and knees. This condition occurs in about 20 percent of pregnancies in women with lupus and can threaten the lives of the mother and baby if not treated. If preeclampsia progresses to eclampsia, the mother is likely to experience seizures, unconsciousness, and possibly even death. Doctors may have to perform an emergency caesarian section to save the baby if this happens.

Some women with lupus have antiphospholipid antibodies in their blood, and this too poses a pregnancy risk. Women with this type of antibody are at risk of developing blood clots in the blood vessels and in the placenta. Most doctors try to prevent this from happening by prescribing aspirin or another blood thinner for the patient.

Women with lupus, even when well controlled, are at greater risk than normal for having a baby that is premature or stillborn, so physicians must constantly monitor the condition of both mother and fetus. The offspring of lupus patients have a greater than normal chance of developing the disease, so this is also a consideration in deciding whether or not to have children. Some babies born to mothers with lupus are born with heart defects or with neonatal lupus, so this risk too must be considered.

Other Lifestyle Issues

Lupus requires many other changes and considerations in day-to-day living for many patients. Some people with the disease have a hard time dealing with the disturbing physical changes such as a prominent malar rash, skin lesions, hair loss, or weight gain. As one patient put it, "I know that it may sound vain, but sometimes the thing that gets to me the most is how lupus has changed my looks. It's hard not to be upset by the fact that when I look in the mirror, I don't recognize my own face."[28] There are some things patients can do to try to diminish these changes to their appearance. There are cosmetics that

Lupus patients should eat a well-balanced, low-fat diet that includes fruits, vegetables, and whole grains.

cover rashes. Patients who are uncomfortable with hair loss from lupus or as a side effect of medications can wear a wig or cover their heads with a turban, scarf, or hat. Those who get excessive facial hair as a side effect of steroids can bleach the hair, use a chemical depilatory (hair remover) sold in drug stores, or undergo waxing or electrolysis treatments.

Those who gain weight (often a result of taking steroids) can benefit emotionally and physically from losing weight, as Valerie, a lupus sufferer, reveals:

> I lost twenty-four pounds by reducing fat and increasing my intake of vitamins and potassium (fruits like bananas and oranges). I have fewer pains in my knees because of this weight loss, and the vitamins seem to reduce the butterfly rash on my face. Who knows if diet helps lupus, but if you carry too many pounds the pain is certainly greater. And now I feel better with other people, because I feel pretty in my new body. It's a morale booster.[29]

Even lupus patients who are not overweight should be concerned with diet. Doctors recommend a well-balanced, nutritious diet so patients stay as healthy as possible. This includes foods low in fats and high in fiber. People with lupus must be conscious of their fat and protein intake, as they are at higher than normal risk for heart disease, which is often a result of fat buildup in the blood vessels, and of kidney disease, which can be exacerbated by too much protein. It is important that people with lupus also avoid eating alfalfa sprouts since an amino acid called L-canavanine in this food can increase inflammation.

Physicians also say that people with lupus should not smoke at all and should not drink alcohol except for maybe an occasional glass of wine with the doctor's permission. Smoking and alcohol can cause heart disease and osteoporosis, which lupus patients are prone to, and alcohol can also cause gastrointestinal upsets. People with lupus are especially liable to experience gastrointestinal problems such as severe vomiting and must be careful to avoid complications such as ulcers in the esophagus and an inability to eat that may force them to receive nourishment through an IV or through a stomach tube. Patients must also beware of inciting gastrointestinal upsets by eating unfamiliar foods when traveling.

Travel in itself can trigger lupus flares due to unfamiliar schedules and fatigue, so patients who travel must insure that they are prepared for emergencies. Patients must plan for rest time on the trip to minimize the risk of getting overtired and experiencing a flare. They need to bring an adequate supply of medications to get them through the trip, and many doctors encourage patients to bring along antibiotics in case they get an infection. Purchasing trip insurance, which reimburses fees paid when the trip has to be cancelled or cut short due to illness, is a good idea. Doctors also recommend that people with lupus avoid going to countries with poor sanitation or inferior medical facilities because of the risk of becoming critically ill.

Other aspects of living with lupus that face patients are financial issues and discrimination in employment. Costs for diagnosing and treating lupus are high and can reach many thousands of dollars. For patients without health insurance, this can be a burden. Many people with the disease must also stop working, which can worsen financial problems. Some people are eligible for federal Social Security disability payments, but others are not and incur severe financial hardships. Those who are able to work may encounter discrimination such as being fired when an employer finds out about the illness or not being hired because the employer fears frequent absences from work or high medical bills for the company health plan.

It is illegal to discriminate against anyone simply on the basis of an illness or disability since the Americans with Disabilities Act was passed by the United States Congress in 1990. If a person can fulfill the requirements of a given job, the law states that they must be hired or retained even if they have a disability. However, this law is not always followed, and many people with lupus find it difficult to find or maintain employment for this reason.

The Americans with Disabilities Act

On July 26, 1990, President George H. W. Bush signed into law the Americans with Disabilities Act. This was the first comprehensive civil rights law for people with disabilities in the world. The act prohibits discrimination in employment, public services, public accommodations, and telecommunications. It opened opportunities for people with all kinds of disabilities by making it illegal to deny a job, promotion, access to public places, and other rights just because of a disability. Employers must make reasonable accommodations for employees with disabilities.

One example of the application and limitations of the Americans with Disabilities Act concerned a nurse in Kansas who had frequent lupus flares that left her with pain in her hands and back and swelling in her knees. The hospital that employed her accommodated the nurse's disability by giving her a lighter medication cart to push and by assigning her to a section of the hospital where she had to walk less distance. But soon she began calling in sick and missing work a great deal. The hospital fired her, and the courts ruled that the facility was not obligated to keep her employed because they had made reasonable accommodations for her disability and she was still unable to work.

Braces, such as this wrist brace, help patients continue to do their jobs while coping with the discomfort of inflamed, aching joints.

Whether changes must be made in employment status, daily activities, vacation plans, or personal relationships, lupus patients agree that having the disease alters their lives in many ways. Many patients like Pat, a mother with lupus, manage to maintain a positive attitude and go on living a fairly normal life:

Learning how to accept this disease and respect the part it plays in my life has been a slow lesson in survival. But like anything of value, I had to earn the right of passage and work my way through the labyrinth of trial and error. Although we are together on this ride and I respect the power of the illness, for me it will never take the front seat. I embrace it as part of who I am, but it is not what I am.[30]

Others may despair at the way the disease changes their life, but either way, all people with lupus look toward the future with the hope that some day modern medicine will find a cure for this challenging disease.

CHAPTER FIVE

The Future

Although lupus patients are living better and longer lives than ever before, existing medications have many unpleasant side effects and there is still no cure for the disease, so researchers are determined to find better treatments and perhaps a cure someday. Research is also being done on the causes and mechanisms involved in lupus. According to the Lupus Research Institute:

> Lupus needs a breakthrough. There hasn't been a major new treatment approved for this devastating autoimmune disease in more than 40 years. No targeted anti-inflammatory drugs. No refined treatments for lupus rash, kidney disease (lupus nephritis), extreme fatigue, swollen joints, or tools for better assessing the signs and symptoms of lupus. No simplified diagnostic measure to promote prevention. [31]

How New Drugs Are Tested

To address the need for new and better treatments, one area of intense research involves developing and testing new drugs for lupus. New drugs are first tested on animals in a laboratory. Once a compound has been proven safe and effective in a laboratory setting, the drug developer may apply to the Food and Drug Administration (FDA) in the United States or to comparable agencies in other countries to begin testing on humans in clinical trials. A clinical trial generally involves three phases. Phase 1 lasts several months and is designed to determine safe doses and methods of taking the drug and to track any adverse effects that may occur. For example, in Phase 1 doctors determine whether the drug should be given by mouth or by injection. Only a few patients, seldom more than twenty, participate in Phase 1 trials. All are volunteers who are informed that the drug being tested may or may not help them. People volunteer for clinical trials through physicians participating in the study or by contacting research centers that advertise the trials online or through support groups aimed at patients with various diseases.

When Phase 1 trials show that a new drug appears to help people and to be without dangerous side effects, Phase 2 may begin. Here more volunteer patients, perhaps as many as one hundred, are given the new drug to further test its safety and effectiveness. If carefully analyzed test results indicate that the drug is extremely safe and effective, the manufacturer may apply to the FDA for so-called fast track testing status so that the medication can be made available promptly for widespread Phase 3 testing. If, on the other hand, questions remain as to whether the drug is indeed safe and worthwhile for the purpose it was developed, it may be sent back to the laboratory for modification or simply dropped from further trials.

In Phase 3, which can last several years, hundreds or even thousands of volunteers are randomly assigned to either experimental or control groups to test the drug's effectiveness. Patients in a control group are unknowingly given a placebo, or fake drug that looks like the real thing. This control is necessary because sometimes volunteers who receive the placebo in clinical trials experience positive effects simply because they hope and expect to be helped. Thus if results from the control and experimental groups are very similar, scientists cannot rule out the possibility that expectations that the new drug will work, rather than the drug itself, are responsible for any perceived healing. If, on the other hand, researchers determine that a sufficient number of people in the experimental

Food And Drug Administration

The U.S. government's Food and Drug Administration regulates food and drugs to make sure the supply available to the public is safe. Prior to the founding of this agency in the early 1900s, people in the United States were not protected against dangerous ingredients and unfounded claims of miracle cures. As described in "The Story of the Laws Behind the Labels":

> Thousands of so called "patent" medicines such as "Kick-a-poo Indian Sagwa" and "Warner's Safe Cure for Diabetes" reflected both the limited medical capability of the period and public acceptance of the doctrine that the buyer could and should look out for himself. Medicines containing such drugs as opium, morphine, heroin, and cocaine were sold without restriction. Labeling gave no hint of their presence. Otherwise harmless preparations were labeled for the cure of every disease and symptom. Labels did not list ingredients and warnings against misuse were unheard of. What information the public received came frequently from bitter experience.

Food and Drug Administration, "The Story of the Laws Behind the Labels," www.cfsan.fda.gov/~lrd/history1.html

Today the Food and Drug Administration requires labels on prescription drugs to warn users of side effects and dangerous interactions with other drugs.

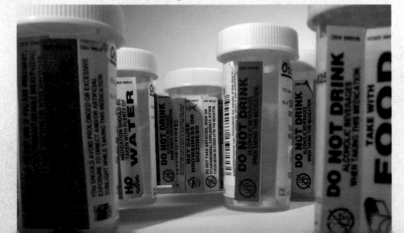

group show marked improvement compared with those in the placebo group, doctors can attribute the positive results to the medication.

Once Phase 3 is completed satisfactorily, the FDA may approve the drug for marketing, and doctors may begin prescribing the drug for patients not included in the trials. Sometimes drug manufacturers then conduct Phase 4 studies that follow the drug's safety and effectiveness over many years.

Special Measures for Lupus

Since lupus patients often have a variety of organs involved in the disease, sometimes it is difficult to measure whether new drugs or existing drugs approved for other purposes are actually helping the lupus. Since the mid 1980s several research centers have developed scoring systems for assessing disease activity, thereby enabling doctors to tell whether a particular agent is helping or hurting the disease process. These measures include the British Isles Lupus Assessment Group (BILAG), the Systemic Lupus Activity Measure (SLAM), and the Systemic Lupus Erythematosus Disease Activity Index (SLEDAI). Doctors hope that the availability of these scoring systems will encourage more pharmaceutical companies to pursue research to find new, effective treatments for lupus.

Research into Monoclonal Antibodies

One type of drug currently being studied for lupus is called a monoclonal antibody. Since many of the problems in lupus are caused by antibodies that attack the body's own tissues, researchers have hypothesized that using specially designed antibodies to seek out and destroy the autoantibodies might help patients. These synthetic antibodies are made by cloning a single antibody-producing cell. One monoclonal antibody being tested for lupus is rituximab. It has already been approved to treat a form of cancer known as non-Hodgkin's lymphoma. Rituximab attacks a marker on the surface of B lymphocytes, which produce autoantibodies. In a Phase 1 clinical trial, researchers at the University of Rochester Medical Center in

New York injected lupus patients with this monoclonal antibody and found that some of the patients had relief from certain symptoms for over a year. Further trials are needed to see if rituximab is indeed safe and effective.

Another monoclonal antibody being tested is LymphoStat-B. This agent hooks onto a protein that stimulates B lymphocytes and it inactivates the protein, thereby preventing the production of autoantibodies. A large Phase 2 clinical trial by Human Genome Sciences showed a significant reduction in autoantibodies and in lupus symptoms after administration of Lympho-Stat-B. The drug also appears to be very safe. Phase 3 clinical trials are underway, and lupus experts are eagerly awaiting the results. Sandra C. Raymond, president and chief executive officer of the Lupus Foundation of America said:

> We need safer and more effective therapies. We will be following the LymphoStat-B Phase 3 clinical trials with great interest, both because of the significant unmet medical need that exists and because LymphoStat-B is being studied as a treatment for the underlying disease of lupus, rather than for the treatment of individual symptoms.[32]

Another monoclonal antibody being studied is epratuzumab, which binds to an antigen on B cells and controls lupus by depleting B cell counts. In a Phase 1 clinical trial of epratuzumab, lupus patients were given the drug every two weeks for eighteen weeks. The activity of their lupus was measured using the BILAG scores, which have been developed for assessing the severity of lupus activity. The scores for all patients given epratuzumab decreased by 50 percent or more, and three patients showed no disease activity by the eighteenth week of treatment, so the drug appears promising.

Other Drugs Being Tested

There are other types of drugs besides monoclonal antibodies being tested against lupus. One medication is called bromocriptine. This drug acts to reduce the release of the hormone prolactin. Prolactin stimulates milk production in a mother following childbirth, but it is also produced in smaller quantities in nonpregnant women and in men. When the level of prolactin is higher than normal, this can lead to the production of autoantibodies. Researchers hope that bromocriptine will reduce the level of prolactin and thereby reduce symptoms of lupus.

Another type of drug being investigated is immunomodulators. These medications suppress the autoimmune response but do not hinder the function of the immune system against foreign invaders like viruses and bacteria. They are called immunomodulators because they modulate the action of the immune system. One such drug being tested is LJP394, also known as Riquent. LJP394 targets an anti-DNA antibody often found in the blood of lupus patients, particularly when they have kidney disease. It is now undergoing testing in Phase 3 clinical trials. So far results indicate that the drug reduces the quantity of anti-DNA antibodies and may also reduce the risk of kidney disease.

Other research on targeting the autoimmune response is being conducted at the University of Texas Health Science Center. Here researchers are attempting to block the body's attack of its own cells by constructing fake targets that B cells can bind to. If successful, this process could stop the autoimmune response that leads to lupus without damaging the entire immune system.

Since kidney damage is one of the most devastating problems in lupus, many researchers are looking for ways of preventing or reversing this damage. One substance that can repair damaged organs is BMP7. It is found naturally in the kidneys, and scientists have made a synthetic form that can be used to repair broken bones. Researchers are now testing whether BMP7 can heal the scar tissue that lupus produces in the kidneys. So far, in mice, it appears to reverse the scarring process and produce healthy new tissue.

In other research on drugs to prevent or reverse kidney disease in lupus, investigators at the University of Pennsylvania in Philadelphia have discovered that a protein called poly

(ADP-ribose) polymerase-1 (PARP) may cause kidney lesions that resemble lupus nephritis in mice. They are experimenting with various drugs that inhibit PARP to see if they can prevent kidney disease in mice with lupus, and, if so, they plan to test these drugs on humans with the disease.

Research on Biomarkers

Many researchers are studying new biomarkers that can be used for diagnosing lupus and for assessing the risk or presence of certain complications from the disease. Biomarkers are substances that indicate the presence or severity of a particular disease. A study by investigators at the Medical University of South Carolina looked for specific proteins in the urine of lupus patients with kidney disease in hopes of using these proteins to gauge how severe the kidney disease was. They found several proteins that can indicate the type and severity of kidney disease in these patients. Until this research was carried out, the only way of analyzing the type and degree of kidney disease was for the patient to undergo a kidney biopsy, which involves inserting a needle into the kidney and removing a sample of tissue for analysis. In the case of lupus patients, kidney biopsies may need to be repeated often to keep tabs on renal disease. The researchers in South Carolina hope that the biomarkers they used (urine proteins) could be developed into clinical tests that would replace kidney biopsies and make assessing kidney damage much easier.

Researchers at the University of California, Los Angeles, are studying ways of assessing which lupus patients are at particular risk for heart disease. It appears that many individuals with lupus have abnormal high density lipoproteins (HDL), a type of cholesterol that usually protects blood vessels from fat buildup. The abnormal HDL does not prevent fat from building up in artery walls, and this increases the risk of heart disease. People with lupus also seem to have increased levels of the so-called "bad" cholesterol (low density lipoproteins, or LDL) and of antibodies to an enzyme called lipoprotein lipase. The researchers are hoping to use blood levels of abnormal HDL,

LDL, and lipoprotein lipase as indicators of heart disease in lupus patients.

Improved biomarkers that can be used to diagnose lupus and monitor overall disease activity are also being investigated. A team of researchers led by Dr. Joseph M. Ahearn at the University of Pittsburgh has developed blood tests that measure the levels of certain proteins on the surface of red blood cells. These proteins are related to the level of inflammation and tissue damage in lupus, and the investigators are studying how well these blood tests diagnose lupus and indicate disease flares. The Alliance for Lupus Research commented:

> Dr. Ahearn's study shows promise for yielding biomarkers that can increase the accuracy of lupus diagnosis, provide better ways of measuring the response to therapies being tested in clinical trials for people with lupus, and allow earlier and more accurate detection of disease flares, enabling better treatment of the disease.[33]

Research into Causes of Lupus

Another important area of lupus research is on causes of the disease. One process that has been implicated in causing lupus is impaired apoptotic clearance. Apoptosis is the normal process by which cells in the body are preprogrammed to die. Each day the human body removes over ten billion cells that die in a mechanism called apoptotic clearance. But in people with lupus, apoptotic clearance does not occur like it is supposed to, and dead cells linger on and are believed to trigger an autoimmune response. A study at the University of California, San Diego, has found that mice with lupus that are treated with a type of antibody that targets apoptotic cells showed increased apoptotic clearance. The researchers are hoping that someday such an antibody can be used to prevent or treat lupus in humans.

Other researchers at the University of Michigan in Ann Arbor have discovered that decreased apoptotic clearance may be at least partly responsible for heart disease in lupus patients.

The scientists found that lupus patients have increased death of cells that line the interior of blood vessels, and when these dead cells are not cleared away, hardening of the arteries leading to heart disease may result. The researchers are studying whether the immune system is killing these cells and whether certain drugs can prevent the process from occurring.

In another line of research on causes, one study looked at the Epstein-Barr virus responsible for infectious mononucleosis as a possible culprit for causing lupus. Researchers discovered that in genetically predisposed people, antibodies produced to fight an infection with Epstein-Barr virus mistook parts of the body for the virus and the immune system began producing autoantibodies to these body parts. The investigators are not sure whether this happens on first exposure to the virus or later on, after the Epstein-Barr virus has been in the body for awhile. Dr. Judith James of the Oklahoma Medical Research Foundation in Oklahoma City explained:

One study points to the Epstein-Barr virus as a possible culprit for causing lupus.

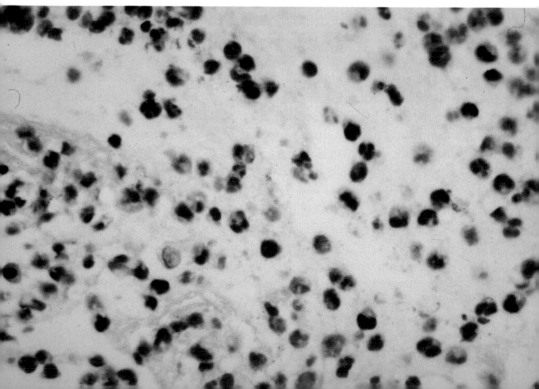

One of the things that is very interesting about EBV (Epstein-Barr virus) is that it is a latent virus. Once you're exposed to the virus, it infects your B cells and is present in your bloodstream at some level throughout your entire life. Different people have different levels at different times. It may be that even if you are genetically predisposed, you may survive and live just fine until the environmental exposure is too high or it reactivates or for some reason you make this inappropriate immune response.[34]

This research may have implications for possibly preventing and treating lupus if a vaccine against Epstein-Barr virus were developed or if medications could be developed to block the immune system from mistakenly targeting body proteins.

Questions as to why more women than men develop lupus has led to research on how women respond differently to various chemicals in the body. A team of scientists at Justus-Liebig University in Giessen, Germany, found that the response of women's white blood cells to a chemical known as TLR7 was greater than the response of men's blood cells. TLR7 led the women's white blood cells to produce more quantities of the cytokine interferon-alpha, which causes inflammation. TLR7 is a naturally occurring immune system protein that sits on the surface of white blood cells. When TLR7 is stimulated by the presence of a disease or other mechanism, this leads to the white blood cells producing interferon-alpha. If a method of blocking TLR7 could be developed, this might be a way of inhibiting lupus in women.

Other research on this topic is being conducted at several major medical centers in the United States. One project found that T cells in women with lupus responded to the hormone estrogen by activating an immune response. T cells in women without lupus did not respond in this manner.

In another line of research on causes of lupus, researchers in Taiwan studying the causes of heart disease in lupus patients found that a protein that causes inflammation and heart disease in people with diabetes may also contribute to these problems in patients with lupus. The protein, known as interleukin-18, was found at higher than normal levels in the blood of people with lupus. Those with high levels of interleukin-18 were also found to have risk factors for heart disease such as insulin resistance and stiff blood vessels. The researchers hypothesize that drugs made to treat diabetes may possibly be of use in preventing heart disease in people with lupus.

Studies on Genes and Lupus

Another area of current research involves studying genes that may cause lupus and that may mediate peoples' responses to medications used to treat the disease. In one study investigators at the University of Oviedo, Spain, are researching several genes that may make some lupus patients more likely to respond favorably to the antimalarial drugs often used to treat the disorder. Patients who respond favorably to these drugs were found to have a specific combination of genes that regulate the production of two inflammatory proteins, or cytokines. The two cytokines are called TNF-alpha and IL-10. According to the Lupus Foundation of America:

> People whose genes made them high producers of TNF-alpha and low producers of IL-10 seemed to be the best responders to anti-malarial therapy. This state of the art diagnostic test could be important to people with lupus. It may be the first of many similar tests that might significantly improve care for lupus patients in the 21st century, by targeting treatments to individual differences.[35]

However, since the study was only done on Caucasians in a particular region of Spain, the Lupus Foundation points out that further research is needed to determine whether the results could be replicated on different ethnic or racial groups.

There are also many studies trying to identify the genes involved in susceptibility to lupus. One type of gene mutation found in people with lupus is in a complement gene called C4A. This gene, when mutated, does not function to remove antibody

The Controversy over Stem Cell Research

Research progress involving stem cells, which have the potential to replace diseased cells, has been slow because the subject has become a political as well as a scientific issue. In 2001 President George W. Bush signed legislation restricting federal funding of stem cell research to stem cell lines already taken from human embryos. Behind this legislation was the belief of Bush and some who share his political ideologies that taking stem cells from embryos destroys a life, because otherwise the embryo would have the potential to mature into a human baby. Opponents of this view believe that the possibility of curing many devastating illnesses, including lupus, with stem cells outweighs the disadvantages of destroying embryos that would have been destroyed anyway. Embryos used in stem cell research are extras made and stored in a laboratory for use in impregnating infertile women. Since they are extras, they would be destroyed if they were not used as sources of stem cells.

The current legislation does not restrict funding for stem cells taken from adults, but experts say that adult stem cells do not have the potential to differentiate into any type of cell as do embryonic stem cells. This has led many scientists and advocates of embryonic stem cell research to argue that the Bush administration policy should be changed.

President George W. Bush addresses the country about his decision to sign legislation restricting federal funding of stem cell research.

complexes, which are then deposited in the skin, kidneys, and other locations as seen in lupus. Knowledge of this gene has led to studies on a synthetic substance that helps to clear out antibodies. This may lead to an effective treatment for lupus in the future.

Other genes found to be involved in lupus are cytokine genes. These genes produce hormones that allow the cells in the immune system to communicate. Some of these cytokines are involved in inflammation, some in the production of antibodies, and others in defending against infection. One hormone produced by cytokine genes is TNF alpha. It has been shown to create inflammation. In people with lupus a mutation in the gene that produces TNF alpha causes too much of this hormone to be made, thereby increasing inflammation. Clinical trials are now underway to determine if a blocking agent for TNF alpha will be successful in improving lupus symptoms.

A gene called complement receptor 2 (CR2) has also been implicated in lupus. A mutation in this gene decreases production of a protein, also called CR2, and low levels of this protein may contribute to the development or worsening of lupus. A team of researchers at the University of Colorado Health Sciences Center in Denver hopes that by studying the role of CR2 they will someday develop treatments that can alter its function to prevent or lessen flares of lupus.

Stem Cells and Lupus

A very new type of treatment being studied for lupus is stem cell transplantation. Stem cells are being investigated as treatments for many other serious diseases, too. Stem cells are immature cells that have the potential to become any type of cell in the body. They may come from a human embryo, but they can also be harvested from the patient's own blood. After they are harvested, the patient's abnormal mature cells are destroyed by powerful drugs. Then the stem cells are transplanted into the person. During the time before the stem cells multiply, the patient is in grave danger of infection because they lack an immune system. They must therefore be kept in isolation in a hospital. Once the stem cells mature and thrive, they replace the diseased cells that were destroyed and enable the person to be cured of the disease. Stem cell transplantation is a risky procedure that is only used in cases where the patient will otherwise die. However, in the future it may be perfected so that many patients can benefit from it.

In one recent study on lupus patients at Northwestern Memorial Hospital in Chicago, fifty patients underwent blood stem cell transplantation using stem cells taken from their own bone marrow. Fifty percent of these patients remained disease free after five years, and 84 percent were alive after five years. Said rheumatologist Dr. Walter Barr, "Fortunately, the majority of patients with lupus can be successfully managed with our available medical therapies. However, for the very severely ill subset of lupus patients who have failed conventional therapies, stem cell transplantation provides a promising new alternative."[36]

Outlook for the Future

The goal of all of this research and many other studies is, of course, to make life better for lupus patients and to ultimately find a cure for the disease. Although this may not happen for awhile, the National Institute of Arthritis and Musculoskeletal and Skin Diseases says that the future for those with lupus looks better all the time:

> With research advances and a better understanding of lupus, the prognosis for people with lupus today is far brighter than it was even 20 years ago. It is possible to have lupus and remain active and involved with life, family, and work. As current research efforts unfold, there is continued hope for new treatments, improvements in quality of life, and, ultimately, a way to prevent or cure the disease. The research efforts of today may yield the answers of tomorrow, as scientists continue to unravel the mysteries of lupus.[37]

Notes

Introduction: No Longer a Death Sentence

1. Quoted in Robin Dibner, M.D., and Carol Colman, *The Lupus Handbook for Women*. New York: Simon & Schuster, 1994, p. 18.
2. Erin Wiley, "Living with Lupus—Dancing with the Wolf." www. lupusontario.org/stories6%20wm.html.
3. Lupus Foundation of America, "Prognosis." www. lupus. org/webmodules/webarticlesnet/templates/new_aboutin-troduction.aspx?articleid=80&zoneid=9.

Chapter 1: What Is Lupus?

4. National Institute of Arthritis and Musculoskeletal and Skin Diseases, "Do I Have Lupus?" www.niams.nih.gov/hi/topics/lupus/tengo/english.htm.
5. Daniel J. Wallace, M.D., *The Lupus Book*. New York: Oxford University Press, 2005, p. 62.
6. Quoted in Theresa Foy DiGeronimo, M. Ed., *New Hope for People with Lupus*. Roseville, CA: Prima Publishing, 2002, p. 21.
7. Lupus Foundation of America, "Introduction to Lupus." www.lupus.org/webmodules/webarticlesnet/templates/new_aboutintroduction.aspx?articleid=71&zoneid=9s.
8. Dibner and Colman, *The Lupus Handbook for Women*, p. 16.
9. Lupus Foundation of America, "Living with Lupus." www. lupus.org/webmodules/webarticlesnet/templates/new_aboutliving.aspx?articleid=13&zoneid=16.

Chapter 2: What Causes Lupus?

10. Mayo Clinic.com, "Lupus Causes." www.mayoclinic.com/health/lupus/DS00115/DSECTION=3.
11. Wallace, *The Lupus Book*, p. 26.

12. Quoted in Philippa Pigache, *Positive Options for Living with Lupus*. Alameda, CA: Hunter House Publishers, 2006, p. 32.

13. Quoted in DiGeronimo, *New Hope for People with Lupus*, pp. 30–31.

Chapter 3: How Is Lupus Treated?

14. Lupus Foundation of America, "Diagnosis and Treatment of Lupus." www. lupus.org/webmodules/webarticlesnet/templates/new_aboutdiagnosis.aspx?articleid=81&zoneid=15.

15. Wallace, *The Lupus Book*, p. 218.

16. Quoted in DiGeronimo, *New Hope for People with Lupus*, p. 81.

17. Quoted in Lupus Canada, "Lupus, Man's View." www.lupuscanada.org/english/living/livingwell_Jody.html.

18. Wallace, *The Lupus Book*, p. 186.

Chapter 4: Living With Lupus

19. Dibner and Colman, *The Lupus Handbook for Women*, pp. 140–41.

20. DiGeronimo, *New Hope for People with Lupus*, p. 221.

21. Quoted Dibner and Colman, *The Lupus Handbook for Women*, p. 117.

22. Quoted in DiGeronimo, *New Hope for People with Lupus*, p. 197.

23. Lupus Foundation of America, "The Adolescent with Lupus." www. lupus.org/webmodules/webarticlesnet/templates/new_aboutindividualized.aspx?articleid=528&zoneid=18.

24. Quoted in DiGeronimo, *New Hope for People with Lupus*, p. 37.

25. Quoted in Lupus Foundation of America, "Kids Speak Out About Lupus." www. lupus.org/webmodules/webarticlesnet/templates/new_aboutindividualizcd.aspx?articleid=506&zoneid=18.

26. Quoted in Lupus Foundation of America, "Kids Speak Out About Lupus." www. lupus.org/webmodules/webarticlesnet/templates/new_aboutindividualized.aspx?a=506&z=18&page=2.

27. Quoted in Lupus Foundation of America, "Kids Speak Out About Lupus." www. lupus.org/webmodules/we-barticlesnet/templates/new_aboutindividualized. aspx?a=506&z=18&page=3.

28. Quoted in Dibner and Colman, *The Lupus Handbook For Women*, p. 105.

29. Quoted in Pigache, *Positive Options for Living with Lupus*, p. 87.

30. Quoted in Lupus Canada, "Pat's Story." www.lupuscanada.org/english/living/livingwell_Pat.html.

Chapter 5: The Future

31. Lupus Research Institute, "LRI: A Champion of Brilliant Ideas and Promising New Investigators." www. lupusresearchinstitute.org/research.php.

32. Quoted in DrugNewswire, "Human Genome Sciences Announces Phase 3 Clinical Development Program for LymphoStat-B ™ in Systemic Lupus Erythematosus." http://www.medicalnewstoday.com/articles/49254.php.

33. Alliance for Lupus Research, "Mining the Complement System for Lupus Biomarkers." http://lupusresearch.org/research/research.html.

34. Quoted in National Institute of Arthritis and Musculoskeletal and Skin Diseases, "Research Shows Common Virus Can Trigger Lupus." www.niams.nih.gov/ne/highlights/spotlight/2005/trigger_lupus.htm.

35. Lupus Foundation of America, "Genes May Play Role in Effectiveness of Anti-Malarials For Lupus." www. lupus. org/webmodules/webarticlesnet/templates/new_empty. aspx?articleid=557&zoneid=76.

36. Quoted in ABC, "Stem Cells Fight Lupus." http://www. wchstv.com/newsroom/healthyforlife/2517.shtml.

37. National Institute of Arthritis and Musculoskeletal and Skin Diseases, "Handout On Health: Systemic Lupus Erythematosus," www.niams.nig.gov/hi/topics/lupus/slehandout/.

Glossary

anemia: A shortage of red blood cells.

antibodies: Substances created by the body in response to a foreign invader, or antigen.

autoimmune: A condition where the body's immune system attacks its own tissue.

anti-inflammatory: A drug that suppresses inflammation.

autoantibodies: Antibodies to the self.

chronic: A condition that is long-term.

complement: Collections of proteins that support antibody activity.

cytokines: Chemical messengers made by the immune system.

erythematosus: Having a reddish hue.

flare: Period when a disease becomes more active.

gene: The portion of a DNA molecule that transmits hereditary information.

hormone: A chemical messenger made by the body.

lupus: Latin for wolf; a disease that affects the skin and possibly internal organs.

malar rash: A butterfly shaped rash on the face characteristic of lupus.

remission: A disease-free period.

Organizations to Contact

Alliance for Lupus Research

28 West 44th Street, Suite 1217
New York, NY 10036
212-218-2840
800-867-1743
www.lupusresearch.org

Supports lupus research and gives information about current research.

American College of Rheumatology

1800 Century Place, Suite 250
Atlanta, GA 30345
404-633-3777
Fax 404-633-1870
www. rheumatology.org

Provides referrals to doctors and educational materials.

Arthritis Foundation

P.O. Box 7669
Atlanta, GA 30357-0669
800-568-4045
404-872-7100
www. arthritis.org

Comprehensive information on autoimmune diseases, including lupus.

Lupus Foundation of America

2000 L Street NW, Suite 710
Washington, D.C. 20036
202-349-1156
www. lupus.org

Offers information on diagnosis, treatment, research, patient support, and local contacts.

Lupus Research Institute
330 Seventh Avenue, Suite 1701
New York, NY 10001
212-812-9881
www. lupusresearchinstitute.org

Sponsors lupus research and gives information about current research on the website.

National Institute of Arthritis and Musculoskeletal and Skin Diseases (NIAMS)
1 AMS Circle
Bethesda, MD 20892-3675
301-495-4484
877-226-4267
Fax 301-718-6366
www. niams.nih.gov

NIAMS, part of the National Institutes of Health, supports research and provides public information on a variety of diseases, including lupus.

SLE Lupus Foundation
330 Seventh Avenue, Suite 1701
New York, NY 10001
212-685-4118
Fax 212-545-1843
www. lupusny.org

Provides patient education, public awareness, and funding for lupus research.

For More Information

Books

Scott Exler, *Loopy Lupus Helps Tell Scott's Story.* Washington, D.C.: Lupus Foundation of America, 2002. Written by a boy with lupus, he explains what it is like to live with the disease.

Philippa Pigache, *Positive Options for Living with Lupus.* Alameda, CA: Hunter House Publishers, 2006. Comprehensive, easy to understand book covering symptoms, diagnosis, causes, treatment, research, and living with lupus.

Internet Sources

National Institute of Arthritis and Musculoskeletal and Skin Diseases, "Do I Have Lupus?" www. niams.nih.gov/hi/topics/lupus/tengo/english.htm.

Lupus Foundation of America, "Introduction to Lupus." www. lupus.org/webmodules/webarticlesnet/templates/new_aboutintroduction.aspx?articleid=71&zoneid=9s.

Lupus Foundation of America, "Kids Speak Out About Lupus." www.lupus.org/webmodules/webarticlesnet/templates/new_aboutindividualized.aspx?articleid=506&zoneid=18.

Teens Health, "Lupus." www.kidshealth.org/teen/diseases_condition/bones/lupus.html.

Index

Picture Credits

About The Author

Melissa Abramovitz grew up in San Diego, California, and as a teenager developed an interest in medical topics. She began college with the intention of becoming a doctor but later switched majors, graduating summa cum laude from the University of California, San Diego, with a degree in psychology in 1976.

Launching her career as a freelance writer in 1986 to allow herself to be an at-home mom when her two children were small, she realized she had found her niche. She continues to write regularly for magazines and educational book publishers. In her years as a freelancer she has published hundreds of articles and numerous short stories, poems, and books for children, teens, and adults. Many of her works are on medical topics.